MORE LEARNING
IN LESS TIME

*Some books are to be tasted,
others to be swallowed, and some
few to be chewed and digested.*

SIR FRANCIS BACON

MORE LEARNING IN LESS TIME

A Guide for Students, Professionals, Career Changers, and Lifelong Learners

FOURTH EDITION

Norma B. Kahn

College of Arts and Sciences
University of Pennsylvania

TEN SPEED PRESS
Berkeley, California

🔟

TEN SPEED PRESS
P.O. Box 7123
Berkeley, CA 94707

Cover design by Fifth Street Design
Text design by Sarah Levin
Type set by Wilsted & Taylor

Library of Congress Cataloging-in-Publication Data

Kahn, Norma B.
    More learning in less time : a guide for students and
professionals / Norma B. Kahn. — 4th ed.
        p.   cm.
    ISBN 0-89815-499-5
    1. Study, Method of.   I. Title.
LB2395.K27   1992
378.1'7'02812—dc20   92-23221
                                          CIP

Printed in the United States of America

1 2 3 4 5—96 95 94 93 92

■ Preface

In its four editions, *More Learning in Less Time* has evolved as a guidebook for an increasingly wide range of students. This fourth edition is written and designed primarily for college, graduate, and professional-school students, and for adults returning to coursework in academic or corporate settings. Most of it is applicable also for advanced high-school students and for anyone engaged in independent or informal group study.

I am grateful to the many generous people who have helped me with all four editions of *More Learning in Less Time*. The contributors I named in earlier editions consisted largely of professors, staff, and students at the University of Pennsylvania from the many years when I was an adjunct associate professor in the Graduate School of Education, and, more recently, my fellow assistant deans in the College of Arts and Sciences. The contributors also included my husband and children and many others to whom I remain grateful.

I would like to thank those who assisted me with the present edition. All contributors, past and present, have helped make *More Learning in Less Time* a comprehensive, concise, and reliable guide.

Professors who recently advised me about effective ways to study in their disciplines are: at the University of Pennsylvania, Bryan Roberts in chemistry, and at the University of Michigan, Marvin Becker in history.

John Kupersmith, who directs computer-based information services at the University of Texas at Austin, advised me about the section on library research. Rhea Mandel, who directs employer-sponsored academic programs at the University of Pennsylvania, assisted me in making the book more helpful for adults returning to college. Diane Goldsmith, who directs education programs for the Wharton School, University of Pennsylvania, helped me make it more useful for business professionals returning to graduate school or continuing their education in business.

Arthur Seidel, Esq., and Harry G. Henn, Professor of Law Emeritus, the Cornell Law School, have generously kept me up to date on copyright laws about which students and professionals should be informed.

Philip Berry and Choti Weiler have helped me realize the extensive audience for this book. Karen Cadbury and Lenore Wilkas have helped me prepare the manuscript for publication.

At Ten Speed Press, George Young has given me the welcome opportunity to revise the book so that it can be of help to more students and professionals. Sharilyn Hovind has ably edited the completed manuscript, and Sal Glynn and other talented people at Ten Speed Press have made the book attractive and readable.

In this fourth edition, as in the third, I include quotations from Isaac Watts's *Improvement of the Mind* (1741), because they reinforce my own statements in more elegant and venerable language and add a historical dimension to the book. *Improvement of the Mind* was based in part on John Locke's *An Essay Concerning Human Understanding*, which was written in 1690 and was among the most widely read and influential books of the eighteenth century. Watts himself was a great English cleric and the author of many hymns still sung today, including "O God, Our Help in Ages Past" and "Joy to the World."

In the preface of the third edition of this book, I expressed my appreciation to Dr. Cyril O. Houle for his book *Continuing Learning in the Professions* (Jossey-Bass Publishers, 1980), and I quoted several passages in it that have inspired me. In the preface of this edition, I want to thank Dr. Houle also for an earlier work of his that is no longer in print, *Continuing Your Education* (McGraw Hill, 1964).

Dr. Houle's *Continuing Your Education* supports many of my own recommendations. I requested permission to paraphrase here its inspiring final passages, in order to extend their benefit to students and professionals of the 1990s, especially adults returning to academic study.

All individuals must answer for themselves, in the light of their abilities, their beliefs, and their ways of life, the question: Why should I study at all? The answer, and the resulting pattern of learning, will change as they grow older. But every time human beings learn, they gain two values: first, the knowledge, the skill, the understanding, or the sensitivity itself, and second, the continuing reinforcement of their ability to learn as their minds and bodies are helped to stay strong and active.

The values of learning, while personally profitable, are not narrowly selfish. Both knowledge and the continuing growth of the mind are essential to society as well as to the individual. Kingdoms and kingly eras were judged by the ability and the wisdom of the king. In a democracy, the people themselves rule—and therefore democracies and democratic eras must be judged by the ability and the wisdom of the people.

I hope that this edition of *More Learning in Less Time* will enhance the ability and accomplishment, the education and wisdom, of active learners from the young adult to the never-too-old.

■ Acknowledgments

The author and publisher wish to thank the following who have kindly given permission for the use of copyright material:

Graduate Record Examination Board, Educational Testing Service, for three items from the 1991–1992 GRE Information Bulletin.

Heinemann Boynton/Cook Publishers and Sandra Boynton for Sandra Boynton's illustration of the quotation from Sir Francis Bacon's "Of Studies."

Harry G. Henn and Practising Law Institute, for excerpts from *Henn on Copyright Law: A Practitioner's Guide*, 3rd ed., 1991.

Leonard Miller, for his questionnaire about test anxiety, copyright © 1979.

Viking Penguin, a division of Penguin Books USA, Inc., for the graphic representation of "Abraham Maslow's Hierarchy of Needs," from *The Third Force: The Psychology of Abraham Maslow*, by Frank Goble, which was published by Pocket Books in 1971, by arrangement with Grossman Publishers, Inc. Copyright © 1970 by Thomas Jefferson Research Center.

Every effort has been made to trace all the copyright holders, but if any have been overlooked the publishers will be pleased to make the necessary arrangements.

■ Contents

Introduction   xiii
Self-Evaluation   1
  Checklist of factors involved in reading,
    writing, and study   1
  Using the checklist   3
  Self-evaluation regarding test-anxiety   4
Organizing Work and Budgeting Time   6
Remembering Effectively   10
**Improving Listening and Note Taking
  from Listening**   12
Saving Time in Taking Notes from Reading   18
Developing Reading Versatility   20
  Reading rapidly for key ideas only   20
  Reading expository material for study purposes   22
  Mastering textbook material   24
  Studying math and technical subjects   30
  Reading fiction or poetry for full effect
    and meaning   32
  Comments on speed reading   37
**Improving Thinking—and Note Taking from
  Thinking—about the Material You Read**   39
  Adapting to reading and note taking in an
    unfamiliar genre or discipline   39
  Taking notes from textbooks or articles in the
    biological or physical sciences   41
  Taking notes from history books or articles   42
  Taking notes from poetry in a first course
    in literature   50

Taking notes from legal cases in a first course
   in law   54
Questioning to encourage critical and creative
   reading of any expository (factual or
   theoretical) material   59
Minding metaphors   61

**Adapting Recommendations in this Book to
Studying Business Cases**   65

Preparing a Research Paper   68
Research   68
Write   72
Revise   73
Submit   74

**Using Four Methods for Effective Study and
Analogous Activities**   75

**Developing a Habit or Hobby of
Strengthening Vocabulary**   77

Learning a Foreign Language   80

Improving Writing   83
Prepare to write   83
Preview   84
Select and chunk   84
Process deeply   85

Preparing for Examinations   90
An example of grouping ideas in
   significant ways   95

Taking Examinations   98
Essay examinations   98
Sample essay question   100
Objective examinations   103

**Improving Concentration, Motivation,
and Willpower**   107

**Keeping Up in Your Profession:
Lifelong Learning**   112

**Keeping Better Informed Through
Newspapers and Magazines**   119
Read newspapers and magazines selectively   119
Preview and select   120

Select and chunk   121
Process deeply   121
Store selected articles, short-term or long-term   122
Adapt your methods to your evolving interests
    and needs   124
Why bother with a system to keep yourself
    informed?   124

Bibliography   127
Appendix   129
Copyright Law: An Increasing Concern of
    Students and Professionals   129

■ Introduction

This is a "ways-to" book, not a "how-to" one. It invites you to try various ways to learn more in less time and to adapt them according to your individual style and purposes. The book is organized and formatted to help you understand it quickly and remember it readily as you try the recommended learning methods. Many sections are segmented and indented beyond usual paragraphing, to make the content that much clearer.

You are likely to learn more from this book, in less time, if you start by looking through the table of contents and marking the sections that most appeal to you and if you try the self-evaluation described below before reading any other part of the book thoroughly.

Then, start reading one of the sections that especially interests you. You might want to continue reading in the order of your interest, or you might want to read from beginning to end. Whatever order you choose, use a quick marking method in the table of contents and in the margins of the sections; for example, use checks to remind yourself of which sections you read and found interesting and arrows to remind yourself of which sections or ideas you want to try applying. (See pages 114–116 for more detailed suggestions for marking tables of contents, to make them records of your reading and guides to action.)

If you are concerned about studying a subject not discussed directly in this book, look for sections that seem applicable for your purposes. For example, to study pharmacology, read the section on "Remembering Effectively" and consider how you could apply the principles to the material you have to learn.

The sooner you begin to read, write, and study more effectively and efficiently, the more you will learn and remember—both for school and for purposes beyond school. Countless undergraduate, graduate, and professional-school students and many experienced professionals have told me that they wish they had known better ways to learn when they were in high school or their first year of college.

Studying efficiently is like swimming efficiently: the activity becomes easier to do and accomplishes much more than merely keeping you afloat. The sooner you learn better ways to study, the more you'll enjoy learning, the more time you'll save, and the more confident and successful you'll be.

Developing an attitude that is both realistic and optimistic is also vital to academic success. Some first-year college students who were very successful in high school assume that college work will be no harder for them than high school work was, and so they make no attempt to improve the ways they study. When these students receive low grades for the first time, they find that the emotional effect interferes with their concentration. Improving their study becomes harder than it would have been if their initial attitude about college work had been more realistic.

On the other hand, some adults who are returning to college or graduate school assume they will find that academic work is too hard for them. They are afraid that they have lost their academic ability or that they can't become strong enough students. These adults need to develop more confidence that their greater experience, maturity, and motivation will help them to both maintain their rigorous schedule and to excel.

Students of all ages and academic backgrounds have improved the ways they study. You can, too.

■ Self-Evaluation

■ Checklist of factors involved in reading, writing, and study

Identifying specific areas in which you need to improve is the best first step to meeting your needs. Recognizing your strengths as well as weaknesses in reading, writing, and studying can increase your optimism about the process, which will help you improve more and sooner.

The checklist on page 2 can help you evaluate your strengths and weaknesses in reading, writing, and study:

1. In the columns on the right, check the factors that seem to you areas of need or concern, either major or minor.
2. In the column on the left, check the factors that seem to you areas of strength.
3. Leave the line blank next to any factor that is neither a strength nor a need or concern for you.
4. Add any additional factors that seem significant to you as strengths or needs or concerns.

CHECKLIST

DATE OF
FIRST CHECK _____

DATE OF
RECHECK _____

YEAR OF LAST
VISION TEST _____

Area of strength	Factors in reading, writing, study	Need or concern	
		major	minor
	Comprehending written material		
	Responding critically and creatively		
	Retaining information		
	Taking notes from reading		
	Taking notes from listening		
	Time management		
	Vocabulary		
	Pronouncing unfamiliar words		
	Taking examinations		
	Writing papers		
	Rate of reading		
	Self-image as a reader		
	Self-image as a writer		
	Tension when reading		
	Preparation in previous school(s)		
	Present curriculum		
	Present instruction		
	Support/pressures from home		
	Coping with present environment		
	Attitude toward reading		
	Attitude toward writing		
	Concentration		
	Self-confidence		
	Willpower		
	Motivation		
	Procrastination		
	Certainty/uncertainty about goals		

■ Using the checklist

If most of the needs or concerns that you checked have to do with problems in reading and study skills (the upper half of the checklist) and most of your strengths are attitudes (the lower half), this guidebook is likely to be all that you need in order to read, write, and study more effectively and efficiently.

If you have checked both skills and attitudes as needs or concerns (especially the attitudinal factors of poor concentration and lack of willpower and motivation), you are likely to need more than this guide in order to improve.

You might best avail yourself of some combination of the aids provided by a university reading/writing improvement service or learning center. These services are likely to include the following:

1. Interviews to help students evaluate their strengths and needs in reading, writing, and study
2. Reading/writing/study improvement courses
3. Individual tutoring
4. Instructional materials designed to be used independently
5. Workshops on overcoming test anxiety
6. Referrals for personal and/or career counseling
7. Referrals for tutoring in oral or written expression
8. Referral for vision test.

When you have incorporated many of the procedures recommended in this book into your reading and study habits, recheck the checklist. Use a different color pen or a different symbol so that you can easily compare your present self-evaluation with your earlier one.

If your present self-evaluation indicates that attitudinal factors still contribute to your reading or study problems, consultation with a counseling psychologist is probably desirable. If your self-evaluation indicates that skill factors still contribute to your reading or study problems, consultation with a reading/writing/study specialist at a university learning center should be helpful.

If you have strong fears about taking examinations and aren't sure whether you should consult a professional about them, use the following self-evaluation regarding test-anxiety, which was developed by Dr. Leonard Miller, associate director and chief psychologist at the University of Pennsylvania Counseling Service.

■ Self-evaluation regarding test-anxiety*

There are many reasons that account for students not doing well on examinations: for example, being unprepared, feeling ill, missing an important lecture or assignment, distracting noise in or around the testing room, and so forth. Some students do not do well on examinations because they become overly tense and "test-anxious."

If you answer "yes" to many of the following questions, you may have "test-anxiety." If so, you should seek help as soon as possible from a mental health professional who is trained to help people control their anxiety.

1. Do you block or freeze when studying for an exam?
2. Do you go blank during exams?
3. Do you frequently forget information that you previously learned?
4. Do you find the words meaningless as you read test questions?
5. Do you need to reread test questions in order to comprehend them?
6. Do you find yourself plotting ways to escape from a test (sneaking out, feigning illness)?
7. Do you—before, during, or after exams—have physical symptoms such as rapid heart rate, excessive perspiration, tense muscles, queasy stomach, nausea?
8. Do you have difficulty maintaining concentration while studying or taking exams?
9. Do you panic as time runs out during an exam?
10. Do you worry about how you are doing on an exam compared to others taking it?
11. Do you worry about failing an exam?

*Copyright © 1979 by Leonard Miller. Reprinted with permission.

12. Do you find yourself wishing you were out of school, working—especially just before exams?
13. Do you panic on a test if you don't know the answer to a question?
14. Do you get distracted easily while taking an exam?
15. Do you find that you get so tired from worrying about exams that you almost don't care how well you do by the time the test comes?

■ Organizing Work and Budgeting Time

Organizing work and budgeting time are essential to effective and efficient reading and study. To take these essential steps, you will need a calendar-memorandum book. If you don't own such a book, or at least a calendar with large blocks for each date, buy one or the other as soon as possible.

Specific suggestions about organizing work and budgeting time are included with almost every kind of reading, writing, and study described in this guide.

Three general recommendations should be helpful at this point:

1. *Keep in mind the useful concepts of "chunking" and "clustering."*

   "Chunking," as used in this book, means identifying the parts or subgroups of extended materials or tasks, in order to accomplish more readily and effectively what you need to do. Chunking can help prevent procrastination and improve concentration and memory.

   Chunking when you read and study is like chunking when you eat. When you eat meat, you chunk by cutting up the meat, then you chew and swallow one bite at a time; when you eat peas, you cluster peas on your fork, then you chew and swallow the group all together.

   Similarly, when you read and study you should chunk and cluster: cut up the pieces that are too large for one bite and group small items for one bigger bite.

To digest a textbook chapter, don't read the chapter from beginning to end. Instead, chunk it by sections. (See "Mastering textbook material" [pages 24–29] and "Studying math and technical subjects" [pages 30–32] for steps to try after chunking.)

To prepare for an exam, gain an overall view of the total material to be covered, perhaps by making a table of contents for your class notes and reading the chapter summaries of all chapters in a comprehensive book on the subject. Then chunk the material and study one chunk at a time.

> When you read and study you should "chunk" and "cluster": CUT UP pieces too large for one bite and GROUP items too small for one bite.

When you have to learn many details, like new words in a foreign language or scientific terms, cluster by grouping about five words that are related in some way; then study the words one cluster or group at a time. Fit such brief study tasks into short periods of time, like when you are waiting for a train.

You can apply the idea of chunking to many tasks you find difficult to begin or to complete, such as packing for a long trip; organizing stacks of many kinds of material that you've accumulated in a spare room; filing hundreds of articles you've clipped from magazines and newspapers; or planning your sabbatical or retirement.

The notion of chunking is useful for simply noting what you have to do each day. For instance, you can write "Call," "See," "Do" at intervals down a memo page and jot down your notes under the appropriate category. Similarly, on separate pages, you can write at the top, in order, each of the next two months and the next three seasons. (I group these pages in my small loose-leaf memo book behind an alphabetic divider labeled "E" for "Eventually.") Whenever you think of something you should do within these periods, write it on the appropriate page. When the time comes to note what you have to do for each day in the next month or season, retrieve your earlier ideas by consulting your lists for that month or season.

2. *Estimate time.*

Estimate the time each chunk of your tasks is likely to require, and estimate the amount of time you have available each day of the week for such tasks. For courses, assume that you'll need three study hours for every class hour. As you look over your plans for a particularly crowded day, weekend, or vacation-with-work, note next to each task the approximate amount of time the task is likely to take. Add up the time periods you've noted and consider the result. You are likely to feel amazed and relieved that the many separate tasks that seemed so burdensome will fit into the time you have available, so you can work more effectively and efficiently—and also look forward to the recreation you'll have time for, after all.

Sometimes, however, you may find that the tasks do not fit into the time available; therefore, some tasks will have to be postponed until another day, weekend, or vacation-with-work. If you will note in your memorandum book when you plan to accomplish the tasks that must be postponed, you are likely to concentrate better on the work at hand.

In estimating the time you have available for academic or professional reading/writing/study, allow for ample and regular sleep. Sleep is essential to maintain your health, to reduce tension and anxiety, and to rest your brain, so that you can concentrate longer and think and remember better.

3. *Safeguard your calendar, reminders, and plans.*

Every month or so, photocopy the pages in your pocket calendar and memorandum book on which you have made recent notations. Put the photocopies in a safe place in your home or office, as backups, to avoid being concerned about misplacing or losing the originals.

■ Remembering Effectively

The following information about remembering supports many of the suggestions in this guide.* If, as you read this book, you wonder why a particular suggestion is made, you will probably find the reasons among these principles.

To remember effectively, whether the amount of material is small or large, you need to develop helpful attitudes and procedures.

These are helpful attitudes:

1. Care about, or be genuinely interested in, remembering the information.
2. Give full attention to what is to be remembered.
3. Impress the information on your mind clearly and correctly the first time you encounter it.
4. Associate what you want to learn with other related information.
5. Think, "I *will* remember." (An intent to remember is essential to effective remembering.)

These are helpful procedures:

1. Think of details to be learned in terms of a related structure, or create a visually memorable structure for them.
2. If there are more than five details, group them in appropriate clusters.
3. Process the information by using several senses while thinking about the information (for example, recite

---

*The information is derived from two valuable sources: Donald A. Norman's *Memory and Attention* (New York: Wiley, 1976) and James Weinland's *How to Improve Your Memory* (New York: Harper and Row, 1986).

aloud what you can recall from the material read, and check for accuracy; write briefly what you recall, and check for accuracy; discuss what you are learning with others).

4. Review the information within twenty-four hours, preferably before sleep.

5. Use mnemonics (devices for remembering) that are significantly, rather than artificially, related to the material to be remembered; for example, a device for remembering the three main elements of good writing is "CUE," which stands for Clarity, Unity, and Emphasis. (See "An example of grouping ideas in significant ways," pages 95–97).

> Think of details to be learned in terms of a related structure or create a visually memorable structure for them.

To remember extended reading material, you should also:

1. Impress upon your memory the *internal* organization of the new material before reading the material further.

2. Connect the information with related *external* information.

3. Chunk the material into units that are appropriate to its organization and contain no more than seven items each.

4. Process the material chunk by chunk (in effect, chew and swallow each chunk before biting off another chunk).

5. Write down and discuss with others your ideas about the material you want to remember.

Note: If there is something you want to *forget*, avoid as many of the above steps as possible.

■ Improving Listening and Note Taking from Listening

Listening, like reading, should be active; it should involve constant thinking, making connections, evaluating. Note taking from listening, like note taking from reading, should include not only what the speaker or writer said, but also critical response to what was said or written. In short, you need to *make* notes as well as *take* notes.

> Listening, like reading, should be active. . . . you need to MAKE notes as well as TAKE notes.

Below are comments from students who have tried the methods of taking and making notes that are recommended in this section:

"By learning to take good notes the first time around, I've saved a great amount of time by not recopying notes, as well as by the new ways I study the notes."

"Going over my class notes within twenty-four hours . . . is much quicker than going over them two months later when it's all from the distant past."

"By using more creative ways to review my notes, I understand and remember the material much better. Before,

. . . all I would do was read my notes over and then I would forget most of the stuff. I would be frustrated because I didn't remember and I would think I was stupid. To avoid that, I often didn't bother going over my notes at all until right before the exam and so I had to cram."

1. Prepare for listening and learning.
    a) When you know the subject in advance, preview or review related reading in order to recognize and organize the main ideas and terms more easily (that is, increase your background in the subject in a way that makes clear its general organization or structure and some key terms).
    b) To prepare for a seminar, recitation, or meeting in which you are expected to join in the discussion, you will need to do most of the related reading in advance. Previewing is not likely to be sufficient, as it might be for a lecture alone. Note the questions that occur to you while reading so that you have them ready for use when you are listening, discussing, and note taking.
    c) Use a large loose-leaf notebook for note taking so that you can rearrange the pages for study purposes, such as comparing, contrasting, and synthesizing the information.
2. Create notes that will provide a visually memorable impression of the organization of the material.
    a) Write only on the front side of the loose-leaf page so that your writing will show up clearly (no writing will show through from the other side) and so that you can rearrange the material without having to flip over pages.
    b) Use deep indentations to impress upon your mind the relationship between supporting ideas and organizing ideas. Most sections of this book include paragraphs that are indented, to make the relationship of the points as clear and memorable as possible. Similarly, when you take notes from listening, indent each subordinate idea about an inch, in relation to the main or "organizing" idea that you have noted above it.

> Use deep indentations
> to impress upon your mind
> the relationship between
> supporting ideas and
> organizing ideas.

    c) In a class for which note taking seems especially difficult, leave blank lines at the end of each paragraph or section so that later you can fill in clarifying or supplementary information.

3. Save time by using appropriate abbreviations and symbols.

    a) For each course or lecture, decide on abbreviations for words likely to be used frequently. Note your code on the top of the first page on which you use the abbreviation or on a page set aside for the purpose. Three examples of abbreviation are:

      p = poetry   rdg = reading
      compr'n = comprehension

    b) In all courses, learn and use standard (not personal) symbols. Consult the appendix of a large dictionary for standard symbols. For example:

$\rightarrow$	leads to or results in	$\therefore$	therefore
$\leftarrow$	results from	$\Rightarrow$	implies
$\equiv$	is defined as	$\not\Rightarrow$	does not imply

    c) In scientific courses, buy a dictionary specific to the subject and consult its list of standard abbreviations and symbols in the field.

    d) *Remember:* Abbreviations and symbols can save time in writing answers on essay examinations—and they are generally acceptable (1) if they are *standard*, and (2) if, for one or two proper names that will be repeated frequently, you indicate a code on the top of the page (for example, T = Tchaikovsky).

4. Include brief notes of any of the lecturer's anecdotes or illustrations that impress you as especially effective.

These can help you remember the information that they illustrate, and they can help you if you need to explain the material to others, days or even years later.

5. Include in your notes useful comments that you or other students make in discussion during the class or seminar, and in the margin next to the comment write the name of the person who spoke.

6. During (and after) listening, note on a separate page your own ideas in response to what you have heard.

   a) Noting your own ideas and questions can prevent your speaking out in class prematurely and can enhance your clarity and fluency in speaking when and if you decide to do so.

   b) Your personal notes can be helpful also in guiding your future reading and in providing a source of ideas or questions for research papers and exam answers.

Review your notes within 24 hours.

   c) Collecting notes, on separate pages, about your instructors' methods can be valuable during courses and in years to come. Include notes about the instructor's approach to or method of thinking about the subject, and try to apply a similar approach or method. Write down the teaching methods and behavior that you found either especially effective or ineffective. Your notes will remind you of methods and behavior you would like to emulate or avoid, if you have an opportunity to be an instructor yourself.

7. Review your notes within twenty-four hours, preferably within a half hour.
   a) As soon as possible after listening, read over your notes; make corrections where necessary; add clarifying notes on the lines left blank; and note personal comments and questions on a separate page.
   b) Underline organizing ideas and key terms with a colored pen or pencil (a small ruler can speed up this process).
   c) Recite aloud, from memory, the ideas you have reviewed.
      1) Recite after reviewing each chunk up to seven subpoints that you noted about a single organizing idea.
      2) At the end, recite the organizing ideas for four to seven chunks.
8. When taking notes from reading material related to lectures and discussions, insert the page references of your notes from reading into the margins of your notes from listening; or, briefly note ideas you gained from your reading on the blank back of the notebook page opposite your lecture notes on the same subject.

*The learner . . . should always recollect and re-
view his lectures, read over some other author or authors upon the same subject, confer upon it
with his instructor or with his associates, and write
down the clearest result of his present thoughts, rea-
sonings, and inquiries, which he may have recourse to
hereafter, wither to re-examine them, and to apply
them to proper use, or to improve them further to his
own advantage.*

ISAAC WATTS
The Improvement of the Mind
London (1741)

■ Saving Time in Taking Notes from Reading

To save time in taking notes from library books or other material that you should not mark up, imagine that every page is divided into five horizontal sections invisibly labeled A to E, like this:

On a double-column page, the first column can be imagined as labeled *A to E*; the second, *a to e*.

Using this method, your reading and note taking for a research paper would go like this:

1. Write on the reverse side of your bibliographical card the page numbers and parts of pages (that is, A to E) on which you find promising material. For example, notations for a paper on ideas for a new English curriculum might look like this:

On one side of the card:

> Whitehead, Alfred North. THE AIMS OF ED-
> UCATION AND OTHER ESSAYS. New
> York: The Macmillan Co., 1957.

On the reverse side:

~~2C~~	18C	33BDE
3A	21A	35E
6C-E	27DE	38-39A
7A	28B	~~47E~~
13D, E*	10BE	57A
14E	~~31F~~	

2. After *finishing* a book (or as many books as you want
   to read before taking notes on the material), return to
   the pages that you have indicated on the back of each
   bibliographical card. Type notes on index cards from
   the material that now seems *essential*. Cross out the
   page notations that you decide are not useful after all
   (see examples above).

3. As you read, continually reflect upon what you have
   read. Make notes about your ideas and feelings about
   the material. For research papers, make notes on separate cards so that you can organize these with your
   other notes for incorporation in your paper.

   For supplementary reading, make notes on full-size
   paper, with page references in the margin so that you
   can include these with your notes on the book's content when you review for exams.

   See the section on "Improving Thinking" (pages
   39–64) for ideas about how you can intensify your re-
   flection about your reading and improve the quality of
   the notes you take on your reflections.

---

*The comma means that some material in the middle of DE should not be
noted.

■ Developing Reading Versatility

Listed below are suggestions for developing a habit of approaching reading in ways appropriate for your purposes and for the nature of the material—that is, for developing reading versatility. To increase your interest, concentration, and speed in reading required material for which you have little or no background, develop background on the subject before the reading. You can do this in three main ways: attend a lecture on the subject, preview and selectively read material on the same subject which is easier for you or has more illustrations, or try to have an appropriate firsthand experience related to the subject.

■ Reading rapidly for key ideas only

1. Every day choose reading material that you want to read but that you are not required to learn, that you find relatively easy, and that looks readable (short lines, clear print).
2. Using the material of your choice, practice the following exercises for about fifteen minutes every day:
   a) Focus on the title of the article. Quickly review what you already know—and think or feel—about the subject.
   b) Preview expository (nonfiction) material by reading the last paragraphs, headings, and/or the first sentence in every few paragraphs—any organizational aids that might provide, in effect, a map of the material.

c) Tell yourself what you know about the material as a result of the preview.

d) Turn the title into a question, or think of a question of interest to you that is likely to be answered in the material. (In reading an article entitled "New Hope for the Slow Reader," you might ask yourself, "What is the new hope for the slow reader, and is there hope for me?")

e) Read, to answer your question, more rapidly than is really comfortable for you. Concentrate on key ideas, not on your eye movements. Your eyes will move faster automatically when you comprehend the content faster.

f) After reading as much as you can in this way (usually after encountering four to seven key ideas), tell yourself what you recall in answer to your question. If you skip this step, you will probably forget what you have read, unless you discuss it with someone that day or have a strong interest in the subject.

g) If you can't remember, your speed may have been

too fast; review the material selectively for a fuller answer.

3. Measure your increasing ability to read *appropriate* material rapidly; for example, consider approximately how much more you are able to read within the fifteen-minute practice period from week to week. (Avoid wasting time by counting words per minute.)

*B*ooks of importance of any kind, and espe-cially complete treatises on any subject, should be first read in a more general and cursory manner, to learn a little what the treatise promises, and what you may expect from the writer's manner and skill. And for this end I would advise always that the preface be read, and a survey taken of the table of con-tents, if there be one, before this first survey of the book. By this means you will not only be better fitted to give the book the first reading, but you will be much assisted in your second perusal of it, which should be done with greater attention and deliberation, and you will learn with more ease and readiness what the au-thor pretends to teach.

ISAAC WATTS (1741)

■ Reading expository material for study purposes

This material includes books and articles listed in bibli-ographies, *not* major textbooks that should be mastered and *not* imaginative literature.

When students are asked to comment on the value of the steps suggested below for reading expository material, they are especially enthusiastic about the time-saving value of previewing. For example:

"'Previewing' is the most exciting word I've learned in years, in that it has saved me untold hours of reading or worrying about articles that I thought I had to read com-pletely but really had little need for or interest in."

"Sometimes I learn all I want or need to learn just by pre-viewing the article."

"Previewing reading material helps me to be more selective in my choices, and I am able to read more material at a faster rate."

"By previewing, I have found that there are many readings that I need not read completely, and there are difficult articles that I can lay aside, when I am tired or not motivated, to read later—and better."

1. Preview the assignment, including:
   a) the preface and/or table of contents
   b) the summary and conclusion (this *alone* may be sufficient for the preview)
   c) all headings or the first sentence in each long paragraph (if the summary and conclusions are insufficient)
2. Tell yourself from memory what you have learned from the preview.
3. Think about:
   a) the purposes of the instructor in making the assignment
   b) the apparent purposes of the author
   c) your additional purposes in reading the material
4. Formulate and note a few questions related to the purposes you have thought about.
5. Read to answer the questions you have formulated.
6. Pause occasionally to try to answer the questions you have formulated.
7. Take brief "notes" *during* reading:
   a) by bracketing in the margins and/or by *very sparse* underlining (if the book is your own)
   b) by noting pages and parts of pages (A, B, C, D, E) from which you may want to take written notes eventually (see pages 18–19)
8. Take more extensive notes *after* reading; include any ideas of your own in response to the material.
   a) For summarizing, take (preferably type) notes from your page notations on full-size paper, with sufficient indentations to indicate the relationships between the organizing ideas and supporting ideas.
   b) For research papers, take notes from your page notations on 3 × 5 index cards or notepad pages.

9. When your reading and note taking are complete, re-read all your notes, *think* about what you have read, and add more notes on your reflections. (See the section on critical and creative reading, pages 59–61.)

*M*nemon, even from his youth to his old age . . . when he came to the end of a section or chapter, he always shut his book, and recollected all the sentiments or expressions he had remarked, so that he could give a tolerable analysis and abstract of every treatise he had read, just after he had finished it. Thence he became so well furnished with a rich variety of knowledge.

ISAAC WAATS (1741)

■ Mastering textbook material

Your old habits for studying textbooks may seem hard to change, but better ways to study can prove so helpful that changing becomes easier than continuing the old ways. Here are comments from undergraduate and graduate students who tried the procedures recommended in this section and evaluated them:

"When I preview a chapter just before a lecture, I find the lecture easier to understand."

"Previewing helps me get into studying and overcome procrastination."

"The skill of previewing and the idea of getting 'the whole' of the structure before reading helps me integrate the details and retain the information much more effectively."

"I was a meticulous underliner, using a myriad of glorious colors. Now, instead, I outline on one page only and save at least two hours per chapter."

Try using one or more of the procedures outlined below, depending on how difficult the material is for you and how thoroughly you should know it. The procedures are like a set of tools from which to select according to your need. You are not likely to need every one of them for every assignment.

Within twenty-four hours *before* a lecture on the subject:

1. Preview the chapter.
   a) Ask yourself, "What do I already know about the subject of this chapter?"
   b) Read a portion of the table of contents to see how this chapter is related to the ones preceding and following it.
   c) Read the summary of the chapter (usually to be found near the end or at the beginning). If the summary seems clear and full, skip items (d) and (e) below.
   d) If the summary seems inadequate, read all the headings in the chapter and/or the first sentence in every long paragraph.
   e) Study (learn all you can from) pictures, maps, and other graphic aids.
   f) After each step above, ask yourself, "What do I know about the subject now?" and quickly recite your answer to yourself. Check back for accuracy.

Within twenty-four hours *after* a lecture on the subject review your notes from the lecture, preferably within a half hour (see "Improving Listening and Note Taking from Listening," pages 12–16).

2. Question and read each section of the chapter.
   a) Establish a purpose for reading each section. Either make up a question to keep in mind as you read the section (this can be the heading restated as a question, like "What in heaven's name *are* Double Stars?"), or read one of the problems listed at the end of the chapter (as in math and chemistry textbooks).

> Establish a PURPOSE
> for reading each section
> of a chapter. . . . Read to
> answer a question or
> solve a problem.

   b) Read to answer the question or to solve the problem. (If the material is very difficult, read the first sentence in every paragraph of the section before reading the section fully.)
3. Recite.
   a) Tell yourself, in your own words and from memory, the answer to the question you kept in mind as you read (plus anything else you remember from the section), or solve the problem.
   b) If you can't remember adequately, skim the section again and recite again.
   c) Continually tell yourself, "I *will* remember."
4. Write.
   a) After reading (and reciting) each section, note the main point (the organizing idea, perhaps just the heading) of the section.
      1) Indent deeply to show the relationship between main ideas and subideas and to create a visually memorable outline or "map" of the chapter.
      2) Keep your notes so brief that they fit easily on one page (or one page for every twenty to twenty-five pages of text); your notes are to serve simply as a cue-sheet to aid your memory.

3) If the book is your own, underline a *few* words and bracket the most important lines in the section. Avoid the temptation to highlight line after line of type with a yellow marker. Heavy highlighting is actually a procrastination technique; it usually means "This is what I should learn eventually—but not now." Students who overuse highlighting usually think little and remember little about the material they read. They often end up cramming for exams, and they are likely to forget quickly most of the information.

4) Note in the margins of your lecture notes the pages in your texts that are on the same subject.

Continually tell yourself,
"I WILL remember."

b) On another sheet of paper, write down any questions that come to your mind about the material or any new insights you may have on this or other related subjects. Keep in mind: Previewing and making a one-page outline will provide you with a map of the chapter's subject. Like any map, it might contain errors. Also, other maps of the same subject may be needed to provide different kinds of information and a different perspective on the same territory.

5. Review and reflect. When you have completed the chapter (and the one-page outline), reread the outline, underline the main points, and recite as much as you can from memory. Again, reflect, and add any new ideas to the sheet of paper that is separate from the outline. Noting your ideas and questions can help you in your further reading, as well as in your class discussions.

To summarize, here is the rack of tools* with which to master a textbook chapter. To remember all the steps, use the formula "PQ6R"—Preview, Question, Read, Recite, Write, Review, Reflect, Review.

TOOLS	CHECK IF USED
Preview (survey) the whole chapter; recite from memory what you have learned from the preview.	☐
Question (set a purpose: formulate a question or read one of the problems listed).	☐
For each chapter section	
Read one section (chunk) to answer the question or to solve the problem. Bracket main ideas in the margin.	☐
Recite your answer to the question or solve the problem.	☐
Write a line or two toward forming a one-page outline of the whole chapter.	☐
After finishing the chapter	
Review the completed one-page outline. Recite it from memory.	☐
Reflect critically and creatively. Write brief notes about your reflections and questions on a page separate from the one-page outline.	☐
Review the one-page outline again within twenty-four hours.	☐

---

* Most of these steps are derived from the procedure originally devised by Francis P. Robinson and described in his book *Effective Study*, rev. ed. (New York: Harper and Row, 1961).

■ Studying math and technical subjects

Studying mathematics and technical subjects such as engineering primarily involves solving problems. How can you learn more in less time in these subjects?

1. Find and impress upon your memory a structured overview of the material that you have to learn.
   a) Before starting work on the first problems in a course, preview and read the introductory or summary chapter of the textbook.
   b) Before reading all subsequent chapters, study the organizational aids in the chapter—the summary, the headings, and the graphic material that can give you a visually memorable "map" of the whole chapter.
2. Follow the chronology recommended in the section "Mastering textbook material" (pages 24–28): Preview the chapter within twenty-four hours before the class on the same subject, thus impressing on your mind a structure and terminology that will help you take good lecture notes; attend the lecture; then, within twenty-four hours, while the lecture is fresh in your mind, review your lecture notes and study the chapter in the way described below.
3. Study the chapter in appropriate chunks—usually one problem per chunk.
   a) Studying a chapter in a math or engineering textbook would go like this:
      1) Read the first problem, or the first assigned problem, at the end of the section or chapter.
      2) Read the explanatory section until you think you can work the problem.
      3) Work the problem.
      4) Proceed similarly through the rest of the chapter; read the next assigned problem, read the explanatory section of the text, and work the problem—so that when you have finished the chapter you have also finished the assigned problems.

      Most textbooks requiring problem solving, especially engineering texts, have many examples of one kind of problem. Solving all of them would be unnecessary and far too time-consuming. If you can easily follow the sample problems within the first section of the chapter, you should not have to work more than one of each kind of problem.

b) Studying a chapter in a textbook on organic chemistry or physics would be similar, but with some exceptions:

1) Read the sample problem at the end of one section, read the section, then work the sample problem. Wait until you have finished studying all the sections in the chapter before you read and work the problems at the end of the chapter.

This way is preferable in these two sciences because part of understanding them is recognizing which concept applies in a given problem, as well as recognizing how a single concept works in different contexts.

2) Of the thirty to fifty problems at the end of the chapter, do two or three of each type (about ten altogether), unless more are assigned.

4. Be very organized in laying out the problems you work.

a) Follow the layout shown in the text's samples.

b) Draw figures and visualize the problem before you work it mathematically. Visualizing the problem is essential to solving it—it helps you understand the problem better and enables you to check one type of reasoning against another. On examinations as well as in regular assignments, solve the problems geometrically as well as mathematically.

> Draw figures and visualize the problem before you work it mathematically.

5. Work with a small group of other students on your homework problems, if your instructor approves. This can give you a vital opportunity to actively use the language of math or the technical field as you discuss how you arrived at your answers to the problems.

You should study in these ways for three main reasons:

1. The more background you have about a subject—background that is appropriately structured—the more readily you can learn, remember, and apply new information about the subject.
2. To remember extended material, you need to learn it one piece at a time, keeping in mind the pattern into which each piece fits. The best way to learn each piece is to use or apply it in an appropriately structured way.
3. Discussing problems with other students can help you learn better in many ways, especially because it involves using several senses while thinking about the subject. It can help you clarify your thinking and increase your motivation to learn and remember.

You will need to cope with elements of the course in addition to the textbook. In math and technical courses, instructors may not always follow the book exactly; in class, they may spend more time on some areas, leave out other areas, and even add areas not included in the book. Usually, instructors assign homework from the problems at the back of the book—but their exams may include problems that are different from those in the book. Ask your instructor for copies of old exams, or see if they are on file in a learning center. Using the old exams, practice applying what you have learned from class and the homework on problems similar to those that you will face on your next exam.

■ Reading fiction or poetry for full effect and meaning

The recommendations below can help you think more critically about literature and also help you find more personal value in reading it. A professor's questions may call attention primarily to the artistic elements of the literature, such as the plot, characters, and setting of a novel; another's may call attention primarily to the author; yet another's to the world that influenced or is reflected in the literature, and so on. You are likely to be more interested and successful in thinking about literature from different points of view if you first note your personal response to it, then note your critical or interpretive response to it, and finally reconsider your personal response.

The personal values for which you may read literature include entertainment, self-understanding, understanding others, inspiration to change society, and beauty. While all of these values can be derived from most good literature, the values of a particular literary piece may be different for each reader. This is because readers naturally bring different experiences, interests, and needs to reading the same piece, and thus respond in different ways emotionally, imaginatively, and intellectually.

1. Consider—and note in writing—during and after reading fiction or poetry:
   a) the effect of the fiction or poetry on you—emotionally, imaginatively, and intuitively, as well as intellectually;
   b) the scenes, lines, phrases, and images that impressed you most.

> Note the effect that the fiction or poetry has on you.

2. Tentatively and briefly, try to answer the following questions (knowing that you will answer them again when you have studied the work more thoroughly):
   a) Considering the novel, short story, or poem as a whole, what do you think it means? In brief, what seem to be its themes? State the themes carefully, avoiding statements that are too narrow or too broad.
   b) What view of life, or attitude toward life, does the

novel, story, or poem reveal? What is your reaction
to this view or attitude?
c) What is the value of the novel, story, or poem to you
personally? Have you found it entertaining? Have
you found beauty in it? Has it helped you understand yourself or others? How has the experience of
reading it changed you—your attitudes, your feelings, your thinking?
d) What experiences have you had and what tendencies do you have as a reader that might be affecting
your response?
e) What might be the value of this work of art to others? Could it help to change society?
3. If you wish or need to understand the fiction or poetry
more fully, analyze it in detail. Consider how each element of the work contributes to its total effect and
meaning. A work of art is organic, like a tree or a person; in analyzing it, you need to consider how each
element that composes it relates to other elements and
to the whole. For detailed questions that might help
you analyze fiction, see the pages immediately following. For taking notes to support your analysis, use the
time-saving ABCDE method described previously. For
notes that might help you analyze poetry, see page 50.
(After analyzing the novel, story, or poem in detail,
consider again points 1 and 2 above.)
4. Consult one of the following sources on the subject:

Barnet, Sylvan. *A Short Guide to Writing About Literature*. 5th ed. Glenview, IL: Scott Foresman, 1985.

Boynton, Robert W., and Maynard Mack. *Introduction
to the Poem*. 3rd ed. Portsmouth, NH: Heinemann
Boynton/Cook, 1985.

Scholes, Robert, et al. *Elements of Literature: Poetry,
Drama, Essay, Film*. New York: Oxford University Press,
1986.

5. In analyzing a work of fiction, consider the following
elements:
a) Point of view
1) Is the story told by the author, who knows all?

Or through one of the characters? Or through several of the characters?

2) Does the narrator seem to be reliable and truthful? If not, why not?

3) What does the point of view contribute to the total meaning of the novel?

b) Plot

1) What is the scope of the novel in time?

2) What are the major scenes?

3) Does the action seem to develop because of the nature of the characters? Or through societal forces? Or through fate?

4) What is the shape of the story line? Is it a journey or quest? A fall or rise in morals or in fortune? Or a rise and fall? A meeting or marriage? A growing up through experience? An interweaving of story lines?

5) Does the plot have an underlying pattern?

6) What does the plot contribute to the total meaning of the novel?

c) Characters

1) Are the characters "flat"? (Can they be described fully in a few words? Do they change very little in the novel?) Or are they "round"? (Are many of their qualities revealed? Do they develop during the novel?)

2) Which characters are most memorable to you? Why?

3) How are the characters revealed? By what they say and do? By what the narrator says and thinks? By what other characters say? By what the author says directly to the reader?

4) Do any of the characters contrast with one another in significant ways?

5) What do the characters contribute to the total meaning of the novel?

d) Setting

1) What is the scope of the novel in space or setting?

2) Does the setting seem important to the characters? To the plot?

       3) What does the setting contribute to the total meaning of the novel?

  e) Language or diction

       1) Is the novel composed largely of conversation? Does the conversation seem true to life?

       2) Is the novel simply a reporting of events?

       3) Is the novel written with poetic imagery? What are the central images or metaphors?

       4) What is the nature of the diction (the selection of words)? Is it formal? Informal? Colloquial? Slang? Does it change in the course of the novel?

       5) What does the language or diction contribute to the total meaning of the novel?

  f) Tone (a quality of style that reveals or creates attitude, like "tone of voice")

       1) Is the tone of the novel humorous? Serious? Sarcastic? Grim? Lofty? Conversational? How can you tell?

       2) What does the tone of the novel contribute to its total meaning?

  g) Title

       1) How does the title relate to, or clarify, the total meaning of the novel?

6. Which of the elements of the novel seems to be the most important?

7. Now return to items 1 and 2 in this section and add to your original responses to the novel.

8. To enhance your appreciation of the fiction or poetry, listen to recordings of it that may be available in a library or store or by mail order.

For more recommendations about reading literature, see "Taking notes from poetry in a first course in literature" on pages 50–54.

■ Comments on speed reading

Reading rate is an attitude, a mental tendency, which is seldom improved permanently by external pressure of any kind. Machines and other external devices (for example, a moving hand) designed to increase reading speed are not clearly better than other methods, and they have the major disadvantage that when readers who use external devices read without them, they soon tend to return to their former rate of reading.

The disadvantages of speed reading include the following:

1. The pressure to read faster tends to increase the anxiety of students who are already anxious about their reading assignments. As anxiety increases, comprehension usually decreases.
2. Most readers cannot concentrate on their eye movements and on the content of what they are reading at the same time. Therefore, concentration on faster, smoother eye movements usually results in reduced concentration on the content of the reading material.
3. Speed reading does not insure clear and accurate initial learning; therefore, it often creates the time-consuming problem of unlearning and relearning.

Improvement in reading speed as well as comprehension is likely to be greater and more lasting if readers try to improve their central processes (perception, comprehension, assimilation) rather than their peripheral processes (eye movements—see Tinker below).

Subvocalization, or saying each word silently during reading, can help some readers comprehend or appreciate better what they read. While subvocalization was once considered a crutch to be avoided, it is now recognized to be a natural way for some readers to cope with material they find difficult. When readers have more background, confidence, and interest in their reading material, they usually find that they no longer subvocalize, except to appreciate more fully a literary passage or other good writing.

Reading versatility is far more desirable than reading speed. Reading versatility means the ability to adapt reading approach (including rate) to the nature of the reading material and the purpose for which one is reading it. Improvement in reading versatility usually comes with increased background in the subjects about which one usually reads, and with increased attention to setting purposes before beginning to read any material.

> Reading versatility is far more desirable than reading speed.

For further information on speed reading, consult the following:

Tinker, Miles A. "Role of Eye Movements in Improving Reading," *Bases for Effective Reading*. Minneapolis: University of Minnesota Press, 1965, pp. 105–112.

Whimbey, Arthur, and Jack Lochhead. "Six Myths about Reading." *Problem Solving and Comprehension*. 4th rev. ed. Hillsdale, NJ: L. Erlbaum Assocs., 1986.

C lear and distinct apprehension of the things which we commit to memory," is necessary in order to make them stick and dwell there. . . . If we would treasure up the ideas of things, notions, propositions, arguments and sciences, these should be recommended also to our memory by clear and distinct perception of them. Faint glimmering and confused ideas will vanish like images in twilight.
ISAAC WATTS (1741)

■ Improving Thinking— and Note Taking from Thinking—about the Material You Read

■ Adapting to reading and note taking in an unfamiliar genre or discipline

A major problem when reading and note taking in a relatively unfamiliar genre or discipline is deciding what to look for and note as significant. How should you read and take notes from poetry assigned in one of your first literature courses? From legal cases in one of your first law courses? From material assigned in a higher level history or physiology course when you have not had an introductory course in these disciplines? Before considering some specific answers to these questions, consider the following general points:

1. Mere reading or reading and making marks on the page is not an appropriate way to read to learn. To follow many of the principles and procedures of remembering (listed on pages 10–11), reading to learn should include making notes of your critical and creative thoughts as they occur to you and taking notes from the content of the material only when you are fairly sure of what is most significant. (Such delayed note taking is described on pages 18–19.)

2. If you encounter a word, phrase, sentence, or paragraph you don't understand, pencil a question mark in the margin of the book and keep reading. When you've

come to the end of the material and you return to the question marks, you're likely to have enough perspective and information to comprehend the questioned material more quickly than if you had puzzled over it on the first encounter.

3. Don't be surprised or concerned if your reading in the new genre or discipline is much slower and more laborious than in more familiar material. As your familiarity with the new field increases, your comprehension is likely to be quicker and greater. Moreover, freeing yourself of anxiety about being a "slow reader" or "poor reader" will help raise your comprehension; usually, the higher one's anxiety, the lower one's comprehension.

> Mere reading or reading and making marks on the page is not an appropriate way to read to learn.

4. Most important, find out from authorities in the genre or discipline unfamiliar to you what basic questions or structure might guide your initial reading and note taking. One authority could be a professor in the discipline, who might offer guidance in class or conference. You can also analyze lectures to perceive questions that can guide your reading. Another authority could be a basic current text in the field, or a practitioner or expert beyond the classroom.

5. By starting with a basic current text, you are likely to increase your background in the subject enough that you can read more advanced materials with greater ease. You can read the basic texts selectively; the methodology section and the summary chapter or individual chapter summaries may be sufficient for the purpose of guiding further reading.

For comprehensive recommendations about reading and writing in an unfamiliar discipline or genre, consult a handbook written by an authority in the discipline or genre, for example, *Handbook for Research in American History*, by Francis Paul Purcha (Lincoln: University of Nebraska Press, 1987) for history, or *Psychological Research: An Introduction*, by Arthur J. Bachrach (New York: Random House, 1981) for psychology.

As in all reading and listening, maintain a critical attitude in finding and following a basic structure or questions to guide your reading; that is, be aware that another authority may disagree with the one you've consulted and that you can bring from your own knowledge and experience ideas for expanding or modifying the structure or questions you find.

*I*n the beginning of your application to any new subject, "be not too uneasy under present difficulties that occur, nor too importunate and impatient for answers and solutions to any questions that arise." Perhaps a little more study, a little further acquaintance with the subject, a little time and experience will solve those difficulties, untie the knot, and make your doubts vanish . . .

ISAAC WATTS (1741)

■ Taking notes from textbooks or articles in the biological or physical sciences

In the biological and physical sciences, authorities generally agree about methodology; therefore, almost any authoritative text designed to be an introduction to the science would be appropriate as a source of a structure or questions to guide initial reading. However, before taking an advanced course in the science, a student new to the field will be able to learn more in less time by selectively reading not only an introductory text to the science but also introductory material regarding the specific area that is the subject of the course.

To study scientific material, follow the suggestions recommended on pages 24–28 for mastering textbook material; in the "reflecting" step, answer the "critical and creative questions" on page 60 that seem most appropriate for your purposes and for the material. For recommendations about studying physics and chemistry, see "Studying math and technical subjects" on pages 30–32.

■ Taking notes from history books or articles

In history, as in many other disciplines, there are controversies among authorities that should affect critical reading in the field. One of the major controversies among historians today is about whether primary attention should be given to studying the ruling people at the top of society or the common people at the bottom; that is, historians disagree about whether to study history "from the top down or the bottom up."

A more long-standing controversy, which is still current among historians, is about methodology. The controversy centers on a difference of opinion among historians about whether history should be classified as one of the humanities or as one of the social sciences. Historians who classify history as one of the humanities tend to regard narrative as the primary method of writing history; those who classify history as a social science tend to regard analysis as the primary method. Students for whom history is an unfamiliar discipline should keep this major difference of opinion in mind as they read history and perhaps modify the structure or questions that they gain from any one authority to guide their initial reading.

To illustrate, when I asked a history professor to recommend an authoritative book that might guide initial reading of history, I was directed to *Doing History* by J. H. Hexter (Indiana University Press, 1971). When I consulted two more historians for additional ideas to include in this section, I learned that Dr. Hexter's view represents one side of a controversy among historians regarding the relative value of analysis, statistical evidence, and the social sciences in "doing history." Therefore, in using my notes from *Doing History* as a guide in reading history (in this case, *The Emergence of the American University*), I gave more weight to analysis, statistical evidence, and the social sciences than Hexter implies is necessary.

Following are my notes from *Doing History*, a description of the process by which I took notes from one section of *The Emergence of the American University*, and the notes themselves.

Notes from *Doing History* by J. H. Hexter
(Indiana University Press, 1971)

Page
ref.

Definition of "historiography" ("doing history"):

15   "the craft of writing history and/or the yield of such writing considered in its rhetorical aspect" (Hexter)

154   —as a branch of intellectual history: "the history of the ideas of historians about the past"

15   —as a subbranch of the sociology of knowledge: "the history of history writing."

Thesis: "The communication and therefore the advancement of historical knowledge is inseparable

44

from the rhetoric of history"; in other words, historians convey knowledge of the past at once by what they write and by the way they write.

Basic questions and subquestions that can be derived from *Doing History* to guide initial reading of history:

A. How (and how well) has this historian "done" history? (Only "provisional judgments" are possible, even with knowledge of the historical record.)

51

1. Does the historian communicate what-happened-and-how by historical narrative, historical analysis, or both, organically integrated?

   a) Narrative (telling a story or stories) is "the principle of coherence traditionally and still most generally employed" by historians.

27

   b) Analysis requires formulation of a rough hypothesis "for which the surviving records hold forth some hope of verification."

2. How "slight or abundant" is the historical evidence, how "adequate or inadequate" the historical proof?

   a) Does the evidence include quantification, statistical foundations? (e.g., "one-fortieth of the population" instead of "a tiny fraction"?)

142

3. To what extent does the historian use material from the social sciences?

4. To what extent is this history comparative, as opposed to nationalistic or ethnocentric?

5. To what extent is the language denotative, to what extent connotative?

   a) Denotative language of historiography is like that of the natural sciences; it may be desirable and necessary to make accounts more complete, exact.

   Major difference between use of denotative language in history and in natural

57   sciences: "to convey historical reality. . . . with maximum impact . . . may require a historian to subordinate completeness, explicitness, and exactness to other considerations."

        b) Connotative ("evocative and even metaphorical") language of historiography is "nearer to the language of the fictive arts"; it "may be desirable and even necessary," in order to bring the reader "into confron-

43   tation with events long past and men long dead," to make accounts "forceful, vivid, lively."

        Major difference between use of connotative language in history and in fictive arts: the "overriding commitment

47   of historians to fidelity to the surviving records of the past."

25   B. What understanding of the past ("historical reality") does the historian communicate to me through his writing?
      —what "movement and tempo of events"
      —what "motives and actions of men"
      —what "impact on the course of events of an accident, a catastrophe, or a bit of luck. . . ."?

Description of a Process of Taking Notes from History

Book of history chosen for this description: *The Emergence of the American University*, by Lawrence R. Veysey (Chicago: University of Chicago Press, 1965).

1. I conjectured that the typical assignment in an advanced history course would involve reading from an extensive bibliography (rather than mastering one or two textbooks), that most of the books in the bibliography would be on reserve in the library, and therefore that the books could not be marked and notes would have to be more detailed in order to have sufficient material for review.

2. I read the table of contents to discover the scope of the

book and to locate the pages where the thesis of the book would probably be stated.

3. I looked for a statement of the thesis and elaboration of it in the first and last paragraphs of the preface and the conclusion; when I found what I was looking for (in the first sentences of the opening paragraphs of these sections), I noted the pages and parts of pages from which I would probably want to take notes.

4. Returning to the pages and parts of pages I had noted, I took notes on the thesis, quoting directly for the most part (using quotation marks), because the field is relatively new to me and I did not feel certain yet of paraphrasing accurately and quickly.

5. Looking up from my notes, I told myself the thesis from memory in order to impress it more deeply upon my memory and so help me comprehend more quickly as I read on.

6. I returned to the table of contents to note the main headings that indicate the scope of the book in relation to the thesis.

7. I decided which section of the book interested me most and was therefore the best place to start reading, because it would help me "get into" the book—connect the material directly with my previous knowledge and interests and so increase my attention and comprehension as I read on.

8. I previewed and then read the section of particular interest to me, "The Academic Standards of the New Age," in the chapter entitled "The Tendency to Blend and Reconcile," noting pages and parts of pages from which I might want to take notes.

9. Following the questions suggested to me by Hexter's *Doing History*, modified by what I had learned from other historians, I made notes of my critical response to the section.

10. I took notes on the content of the section. If I were to read the whole book, I would follow steps 8 and 9, then check out the book from the reserve room (overnight or three-day checkout is all that is usually permitted) and type notes from the content, following my notations of pages and parts of pages.

Note: If I were responsible for mastering the material, I would follow the steps suggested for mastering textbook material (pages 24–28) to the extent that they seemed necessary.

Notes on the Thesis and Scope of
The Emergence of the American University

Page
ref.

Thesis

In America, "the idea of the university . . . underwent a process . . . of assimilation to the New
439   World environment, accompanied by profound internal tension and a mingled sense of gain and loss."

"The most striking thing about the American
vii   university in its formative period is the diversity of mind shown by the men who spurred its development."

"The two most important types of academic
viii   conflict in the late nineteenth century were over the basic purpose of the new university and over the kind and degree of control to be exerted by the institution's leadership."

Scope

Part 1:

    Rival Conceptions of the Higher Learning, 1865–1910

      1. Discipline and Piety

      2. Utility

      3. Research

      4. Liberal Culture

    A Season of Reassessment, 1908–1910

Part 2:

    The Price of Structure, 1890–1910

      5. The Pattern of the New University (including)

        a. The Gulf between Students and Faculty

      b. The Rise of Administration
    6. The Tendency to Blend and Reconcile
      a. The Growing Merger of Ideals
      b. Business Models for Educational Enterprise
      c. The Academic Standards of the New Age
      d. Varieties of the "New" Administrator
    7. The Problem of the Unreconciled
Conclusion:
    The University as an American Institution

Notes from One Section*

A. The Academic Standards of the New Age

1. Increasing emphasis on quantification (objected to by some), e.g., Eliot (Harvard): "Quality being secured, the larger the better."
2. "Concern for quantitative success tended to inhibit quality"
   a) Admission standards low in new universities (Cornell, Stanford) to insure numbers
   b) Larger faculty-student ratio made control of academic standards difficult
3. Conflicting evidence re expectations of academic performance
   a) Requirements grew somewhat harder, 1865–1910
      1) More students required to repeat courses
      2) Honors programs instituted
   b) But standards of work very low compared to mid-20th century; e.g., some Harvard students received A's for courses never attended, and only 3 hours of tutoring
4. Improvement of quality difficult because educators disagreed about:

---

*Abbreviations are not included here, in order to make the notes more readable; had I abbreviated, I would have used a code like this:

acad.stds. = academic standards   fac. = faculty   st. = students
tchg. = teaching   u. = undergraduates

a) How "serious" undergraduate work should be
b) "Substantive meaning of seriousness," e.g., scientific vs. humanistic professors; accuracy of footnotes vs. "verbal flair and moral dedication"

Comments on "The Academic Standards of the New Age"

A. Of particular interest and value to me:
  1. The perspective this section gives me on
     a) college admissions problems, past and present (#1 and #2)
     b) past and present need for student services (e.g., learning centers) to help students study more effectively (#3)
     c) current controversy among historians (#4)

B. How Veysey has "done history" here:
  1. Historical analysis; no narrative in this section
     a) Subthesis statements supported by extensive evidence (nonstatistical), with many footnotes to indicate direct sources, additional sources, or additional details.
     b) Example: "The standard of work at leading institutions, despite the upturn of the years after 1905, remained extraordinarily low by the canons of the mid-twentieth century. . . . At Yale in 1903 seniors required only an hour or less per day to prepare for all their classes." (Footnote cites three sources of this and of similar information) p. 357
  2. Language almost entirely denotative (as illustrated in quotation above)

C. Sense of the past conveyed:
  1. From this section, a sense of the past is largely the result of:
     a) cumulative effect of abundant evidence solidly organized in support of points made
     b) naming rather than narrating of "movement of events," "motives and actions of men"
     c) background that most readers are likely to bring to the book (familiarity with at least one American university)

■ Taking notes from poetry in a first course in literature

To improve your reading of and note taking from poetry, find a basic text on literature in general or on poetry in particular by looking through the books required for introductory courses in literature or poetry. You're likely to learn most readily from introductory books that are clearly organized and relatively free of jargon. Examples of such books are: *A Short Guide to Writing about Literature*, by Sylvan Barnet (5th ed., Glenview, IL: Scott Foresman, 1985) and *Introduction to the Poem*, by Robert W. Boynton and Maynard Mack (3rd ed., Portsmouth, NH: Boynton/Cook, 1985).

Your notes from *Introduction to the Poem*, to guide your reading of poems, would probably look something like this:

1. Who is the speaker?
2. Who is the audience?
3. What is the tone (of voice) in which the speaker addresses the audience?
4. What is the subject? The theme? The meaning?
5. What does the pattern of rhythm and sound contribute to the effect and meaning of the poem?
6. What "devices of compression" are apparent?
   a) Understatement
   b) Irony
   c) Paradox
   d) Comparison by means of simile, metaphor, juxtaposition
7. How do these devices contribute to the effect and meaning of the poem?

Your notes on your analysis of a specific poem could follow the structure of the questions above. Consider your notes tentative until after you have reread the poem many times to find evidence to support each of your statements, especially those about theme and meaning.

The authors of *Introduction to the Poem* and authors of other introductory texts on literature probably would agree that *before* analyzing a poem in detail, you should consider and note the impact of the total poem upon you, and that *after* analyzing a poem, you should consider and note the value of the poem for you personally. Questions to guide these initial and final responses might be these:

1. What is the total effect of the poem upon you—emotionally, imaginatively, intuitively, sensually, intellectually?
2. What is the value of the poem for you personally? How has the experience of reading the poem changed you—your attitudes, your feelings, your thinking?

3. What experiences have you had and what tendencies do you have as a reader that might be affecting your response?

Once you have developed a clear understanding of some of the ways that poems can convey meaning and affect the reader, you will be able to read and take notes from poems more spontaneously, without direct reference to a structure such as the one derived from *Introduction to the Poem*.

Here is an example of notes taken on a poem, following the structure provided by *Introduction to the Poem*:

Art

Herman Melville

In placid hours well-pleased we dream
Of many a brave unbodied scheme.
But form to lend, pulsed life create,
What unlike things must meet and mate:
A flame to melt—a wind to freeze;
Sad patience—joyous energies;
Humility—yet pride and scorn;
Instinct and study; love and hate;
Audacity—reverence. These must mate,
And fuse with Jacob's mystic heart,
To wrestle with the angel—Art.

1. Immediate total effect: Sense of complexity of art (poetry) and all that contributes to its creation—forces both within and beyond the artist (poet).
2. Elements (and their evidence in the poem):
   a) Dramatic situation: Artist (poet) at once contemplating the act of creating art and engaging in that act. (Evidence: Literal and figurative meaning of the words themselves—and their embodiment in a poem.)
   b) Speaker: A dreamer and artist, by implication the creator of this poem on the subject of creating poetry.
   c) Audience: Other dreamers. (Evidence: The grammatical subject and verb of the first two lines are "we dream.")
   d) Tone: 1) Heightening awe. (Evidence: The exclamatory fourth line; quickening alternation of various "unlike things" which must mate, from "a flame to melt—a wind to freeze" to "audacity—reverence"; the culminating reference to a mystical story in the Bible.) 2) "Audacious" effort. (Evidence: Quickening alternation of "unlike things" that must mate

and "fuse with Jacob's mystic heart,/To *wrestle* with the angel—Art.")

e) Rhythm and meter: First five lines are roughly iambic (weak, strong, weak, strong, etc.); the next four lines are dominated by speech rhythms; the last two lines return to the iambic. These contrasts support the contrasts indicated by the words: mere dreaming versus the active meeting and mating of "unlike things"; then the fusing "with Jacob's mystic heart,/to wrestle with the angel—Art."

f) Other sounds: The balance created by the shifts in rhythm (noted above) is strengthened by a roughly similar balance in final rhymes: in the first six lines, every two adjacent lines rhyme; the seventh line is unrhymed; in the last four lines every two adjacent lines again rhyme; and lines 3 and 4, 8 and 9 have matching rhymes. The "mating" of the rhymes matches the mating described by the words.

3. Devices of compression

a) Irony: "What unlike things must meet and mate" for the creation of art—and how "brave" and not so brave is the "unbodied scheme" we dream "in placid hours."

b) Paradox: The creation of art requires both an act of love (meeting and mating of "unlike things" within the artist) and an act of conflict (fusing "with Jacob's mystic heart,/To *wrestle* with the angel—Art").

c) Main metaphors: 1) creation of art :: (is analogous to) the act of love by which a child is created (lines 3 and 4); 2) work of art :: child, offspring; 3) muse of art :: messenger of God, the angel who wrestled with Jacob; 4) the artist (poet) :: Jacob.

d) Juxtaposition: Juxtaposed pairs of unlike things suggest the infinite complexity and balance of opposites within human beings and within their creations.

4. Subject: The creation of art (poetry). (Evidence: The title and the literal and figurative meaning of the words of the poem.)

5. Theme: The complex nature of the creative act, re-

quiring all the human faculties and also involvement of and with the divine.

6. Meaning: Beyond the theme, the poem suggests that the effect upon the artist of creating art is in part similar to the effect upon Jacob of his wrestling with the angel—transformation into a better person.

7. Value for me personally: Effect of the poem is the re-creation of the awe of the poet for the creative act and—through my effort to wrestle with the poem—the realization that reading a poem, like writing one, can be a creative act and so can transform me into a better person. Proof of the truth of the lines by W. H. Auden:

> A poem—a tall story,
> But every good one
> Makes us want to know.

(Know, for instance, the story of Jacob and the angel in Genesis 27–33.)

As you read and reread poetry for academic assignments, note any idea or thesis that you could develop as a basis for a paper or an exam answer. The basic structure of your paper or exam answer could be this: Tell the context of the poem, then present your idea or thesis and support it by discussing each element in the poem as it relates to the whole design.

■ Taking notes from legal cases in a first course in law

If you are unaccustomed to reading legal cases (judicial opinions), you could talk with a practicing attorney to learn appropriate procedures and questions that can guide your reading and note taking in this field until you have personal or professional purposes to guide your reading.

A practicing attorney would be likely to recommend procedures and questions similar to those that follow, because they are useful in the practice of law as well as for law-school coursework:

1. Examine the preface and table of contents of your casebook to see the context of the case you are assigned (that is, the area of the law that the case has been chosen to illustrate).
2. Gain some overall view of the case. In an official report, a headnote is usually provided for overview, with one brief paragraph for each point in the judicial opinion. (Don't depend on headnotes for accuracy, however.) In a law-school casebook, which does not have headnotes, you can usually get an overview by reading the concluding paragraph of the case and then reading, from the beginning, the first sentence of each short and medium paragraph and the first and last sentence of every long paragraph.
3. Read the entire case, chunking the material and taking notes after reading each chunk, according to the following structure:
   a) Facts
      What are the facts of the case? What happened between the parties? Note the facts very briefly.
   b) Nature of the action and procedural status
      1) What is the nature of the action? How did the case get to court? Three examples of the many possibilities here are "A sued B for damages," "A was prosecuted by the state for the crime of _____," or "A sued B for injunctive relief."
      2) What is the procedural status of the case? Two examples of the many possibilities here are "A got a verdict of _____," "B appealed the verdict to a higher court on the basis of _____," or "Plaintiff appealed from the granting of a motion to dismiss the action."
   c) Issue or question
      What is the central issue or question raised in this case? (There may be more than one question or issue.) For example, in People vs. Tomlins, the case briefed on the next pages, the central issue is, "Does a person have the right to kill in self-defense when attacked in their own home and when safe retreat is available?"

    d) Decision of the court
        1) What is the conclusion or holding of the court? (The "court" in some cases will be one judge; in other cases, as many as nine judges.)
        2) By what reasoning did the court arrive at its conclusion?
        3) What is the rule of law on which the conclusion is based? (The rule of law usually will be the answer to the central issue or question; it is the legal principle on which the case stands or that it follows.)
    e) Your critical questions or comments
       What do you think about the case?

4. Your notes for each case should be limited to one side of one page or card, and they should have generally the same structure—a) facts, b) nature of the action and

procedural status, c) issue or question, d) decision of the court, e) your critical questions or comments—so that you can compare quickly and directly your notes from many similar cases to draw conclusions about a particular body of law.

5. Buy a legal dictionary to consult for precise definitions of terms that you will encounter in your reading.

Once you have developed familiarity with court opinions, you should be able to read and take notes according to an order or system that is related to your specific purpose for reading a case.

Some law schools may have orientation days that include presentations or materials regarding effective ways to read legal cases. Such materials have been developed at the University of Pennsylvania by Professor Louis B. Schwartz. In his mimeographed booklet, "Studying Law for Fun and Profit" (1978), Professor Schwartz describes first the goals of legal education:

> Legal education aims to develop critical judgment and a particular set of professional skills. Among these skills are careful reading and precise writing, the power to analyze an argument, differentiating facts from opinion, and recognizing the basic premise or assumption from which the argument proceeds.

In the extract below, Professor Schwartz provides a sample of appropriate note taking from a legal case, which in part illustrates the above recommendations and in part illustrates that good note taking by law students can vary slightly so long as the focus is on the *legal issues* involved in the case.

People vs. Tomlins (N.Y. 1914)

Facts: T shot his son in their home. Testified he acted in s.d. and provoked by blows. Judge charged df. had a duty to retreat if possible where there was a reasonably safe means of escape, rather than kill. Jury conv. T of 1st deg. murder.

Question on Appeal: Did the court commit reversible error in so instructing?

Decision and Reasons: Rev'd. because of erroneous instr. No duty to retreat when attacked in one's home. "Flight is for sanctuary and shelter, and shelter, if not sanctuary, is in the home." Ct. follows Ala. decision in holding that it makes no difference whether attacker was another occupant rather than intruder. Dictum that duty to retreat exists only in "sudden affrays."

Error held rev'bl. even tho def. atty. did not object, since charge in effect deprived T of jury trial. Statute allows reversal in capital case where "justice requires."

Rule: Not criminal to kill in s.d. when attacked in one's own home even if safe retreat available and even if attacker also lives in same home.

Comment: Wouldn't more lives be saved if retreat were required in such situations? Query as to duty to retreat *only* in "sudden affrays." Maybe ruling requiring retreat from murderous attack when [person] has means of defense is inconsistent with human nature.

Professor Schwartz then comments on these notes as follows:

> Note use of abbreviations to save time. The "Question on Appeal" and "Rule" are not absolutely essential since it is fairly obvious from the facts and the decision what the questions are and what rule the case could be cited for. Note the quoted words from Cardozo's opinion [under "Decisions and Reasons"]. This was not essential either, but occasionally it is worth taking note of a striking statement which embodies the rule or policy that seems to influence the court. The "Comment" heading is where you put your own original reaction to the decision. *Always carry your thinking about a case far enough to have a definite sense of agreement or disagreement with the court's judgment.* Test the court's "rule" by thinking of cases where literal application would make it absurd. Formulate an alternative rule which might be enacted by statute. Test its possibilities for absurd application.

Be sure to note reference to statutes in an opinion. Did the language of the statute compel the judge to decide as he did? Was the statute intended to codify the common law or to change it? Which were the crucial words that the Court had to interpret?

The foregoing recommendations for reading and note taking in studying poetry or the law are examples of the recommendations you can find for any genre or discipline if you consult an expert or an introductory text by an expert in the field. Keep in mind that notes from the same material could be taken according to different organizations or systems, depending upon your academic or personal purposes beyond basic comprehension. In fact, changing the organization or system can be valuable in itself, because it can result in your having a new understanding of, or realization about, the subject.

Remember that your business in reading or in conversation, especially on the subject of natural, moral, or divine science, is not merely to know the opinion of the author or speaker, for this is but the mere knowledge of history; but your chief business is to consider whether their opinions are right or no, and to improve your own solid knowledge of that subject by meditation on the themes of their writing or discourse. Deal freely with every author you read, and yield up your assent only to evidence and just reasoning on the subject.
ISAAC WATTS (1741)

■ Questioning to encourage critical and creative reading of any expository (factual or theoretical) material

The following questions can serve as a useful stock from which to draw in thinking about and taking notes on expository material. To increase your interest, attention, and memory, your initial question should be, "What in this material is of particular interest to me?"

1. Critical questions: analysis
   a) What authority or credentials does the author bring to the subject?
   b) What does the author state?
   c) What does the author imply? Assume?
   d) Is the argument valid (internally consistent, logical, the conclusions following from the premises)?
   e) Is the argument reliable (supported by evidence, authentic)?
   f) Does the form strengthen or support the content (by being clear, concise, coherent)?
2. Creative questions: synthesis and elaboration
   a) How does the material relate to:
      1) my own experience, opinion, knowledge?
      2) other sources, oral or written, on a similar subject
         —from other schools or other fields?
         —based on other paradigms, models, or theories?
         —by other authors in the same school or field?
   b) What additions can I think of (improvements, more evidence, additional arguments, new questions)?
3. Creative questions: applications
   a) What applications can I think of?
   b) For whom might this have value?
   c) How can this change *me*?

To increase your interest, attention, and memory, your initial question should be, "What in this material is of particular interest to me?"

After you take notes according to a stock of questions like these, select an idea from your notes that you would like to develop or a thesis that you would like to defend.

Whether or not you actually make the oral or written presentation, simply having thought about the material so critically and creatively will help you remember it better and longer.

■ Minding metaphors

Metaphors, one of the "devices of compression" characteristic of poetry, may be found in any writing except purely scientific or mathematical material. Metaphors may cause comprehension problems for readers who are not alert to this way of conveying meaning.

A metaphor (derived from the Greek words for "beyond"—*meta*—and "bear," or "carry"—*phor*) bears meaning beyond the literal level. If you think of the same word as it might be found in purely scientific and in purely poetic material, you are likely to appreciate more fully the way that a metaphor bears meaning.

Consider the differences between the meaning of words like "light" and "fire" in scientific material and the meaning of the same words in poetry.

In scientific material:

> The sun is our most important source of light.
> Fire is the heat and light that come from burning substances.

In a poem by Dylan Thomas:

> Do not go gentle into that good night,
> Rage, rage against the dying of the light.

In a poem by John Masefield:

> Be with me, Beauty, for the fire is dying;
> My dog and I are old, too old for roving. . . .
> Only stay with me while the mind remembers
> The beauty of fire from the beauty of embers.

With these quotations in view, consider language as a continuum from the purely scientific to the purely poetic, as shown in the following figure.

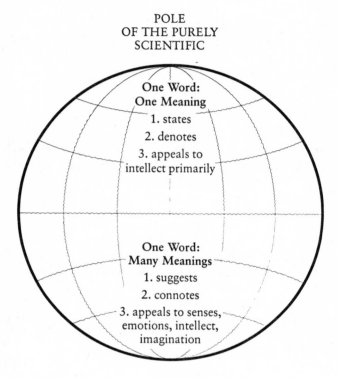

POLE
OF THE PURELY
SCIENTIFIC

One Word:
One Meaning
1. states
2. denotes
3. appeals to
intellect primarily

One Word:
Many Meanings
1. suggests
2. connotes
3. appeals to senses,
emotions, intellect,
imagination

POLE
OF THE PURELY
POETIC

The continuum of language shown suggests that written material may be located at any point from the purely scientific to the purely poetic; that is, that it may be more or less scientific or poetic. In reading any material, especially material in a genre or discipline new to you, be alert to metaphors and the meanings they convey. Also notice similes, which are "figures of comparison" like metaphors, but ones that are usually introduced by the words "as" or "like."

> Be alert to metaphors and the meanings they convey.

Here are examples of metaphors and similes found in material representative of several different disciplines:

History
A historian should yield himself to his subject, become immersed in the place and period of his choice, standing apart from it now and then for a fresh view; as a navigator, after taking soundings off a strange coast, retires to peruse his charts and then emerges to give the necessary orders to continue the voyage safely.

Samuel E. Morison
in *Vistas of History*

Psychiatry
The problem of anxiety neurosis may be epitomized metaphorically as an overactive "alarm system." The anxious patient is so keyed to the possibility of harm that he is constantly warning himself about potential dangers. . . . Almost any stimulus may be sufficient to trip off the warning system and create a "false alarm." The consequence . . . is that the patient does experience harm—he is in a constant state of anxiety.

Aaron T. Beck
in *Cognitive Therapy and the Emotional Disorders*

Linguistics
A game of chess is like an artificial realization of what language offers in a natural form . . . a state of the set of chessmen corresponds closely to a state of language. The respective value of the pieces depends on their position on the chessboard just as each linguistic term derives its value from its opposition to all other terms.

Ferdinand de Saussure
in *Course in General Linguistics*

In addition to such incidental metaphors and similes, basic and pervasive metaphors can be found in almost every field. For example, in the field of English literature, the metaphor of a plant (usually a tree) has been used to convey the concept of "organic form." According to the theory of organic form, a work of art "grows like a living organism, its parts inseparable and indivisible, and the whole being greater than the sum of its parts. . . ." (C. Hugh Holman, in *A Handbook to Literature*.)

Minding the metaphor of a tree can be helpful in trying to analyze a literary work. In the field of psychology, perhaps the most well-known metaphor is that of the computer as an information-processing mechanism comparable to the human mind. In education, the process of education in general (and reading in particular) has for centuries been compared to nourishment, as it is in this quotation from Alfred North Whitehead (*The Aims of Education and Other Essays*):

> It must never be forgotten that education is not a process of packing articles in a trunk. . . . Its nearest analogue is the assimilation of food by a living organism: and we all know how necessary to health is palatable food under suitable conditions. When you have put your boots in a trunk, they will stay there till you take them out again; but this is not at all the case if you feed a child with the wrong food.

■ Adapting Recommendations in this Book to Studying Business Cases

If you read this book critically and creatively, you can adapt and apply its recommendations for reading specialized material or for other purposes not mentioned in this book. A good example is studying business cases.

The term "case," as used here, refers to a kind of professional writing. Business cases differ from legal cases in their form and substance and in their purpose for the reader. Therefore, this book's section on reading legal cases is limited in its applicability to reading business cases. Legal cases are the written opinions of courts, that is, judges. In writing or reviewing cases, judges must follow formal conventions and strict standards, such as the precedents established by earlier cases. Legal cases are read by law students and by practicing lawyers, who must keep up with developments in their fields of legal practice.

Business cases, on the other hand, are published primarily in textbooks for business students. They represent the textbook writer's version of what happened in a particular business situation, which may be actual or hypothetical, and they are presented as problems for business students to analyze. Although business professionals need to be able to analyze situations in their own businesses and need to keep up in their fields by reading business journals, they generally do not need to read business cases unless they take a course for their continuing professional education.

Guidelines that are directly applicable for reading business cases can be found in several sections of this book. The section on studying legal cases is applicable to business cases primarily regarding #2b below.

To study business cases:

1. Preview, read, and take notes, as described in "Reading expository material for study purposes" (pages 22–24), and "Saving Time in Taking Notes from Reading" (pages 18–19).
2. Read critically and creatively, as described in "Questioning to encourage critical and creative reading" (pages 59–61).
    a) To read business cases critically, identify and analyze the most pertinent facts and numbers, which may be both information given in the case and information that you infer from studying it.
    b) To read business cases creatively, ask yourself, "What are the issues in this case?" "What courses of action might be the most appropriate?" "What might be some social consequences, short-range and long-range, of each possible course of action?"
    c) In making notes about the case, include specific examples that support your points, as recommended in "Improving Writing" (pages 83–89) and "Taking Examinations" (pages 98–106). Draw your examples not only from the business case itself, but also from related sources and from your own experience.
3. Prepare to discuss the case in a school or work setting by reviewing the key points in your critical and creative notes.

For more comprehensive recommendations about analyzing business cases, consult Robert Ronstadt's *The Art of Case Analysis: A Guide to the Diagnosis of Business Situations.* 2nd ed. (Dover, MA: Lord, 1980).

Many of the questions useful in analyzing business cases can be applied productively also to a current business problem or business opportunity of your own. While reading and discussing a business case, ask yourself a question like "How can this change me?" "How can my own work or that of my work team on this case be more effective and efficient?" "What have I learned from this case that might help me in my current or future business positions?"

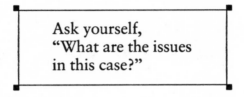

Ask yourself,
"What are the issues
in this case?"

You are fortunate if you have a job in which you can directly apply what you are learning by studying business cases. To learn most effectively, make lists that will help you plan to apply some of the concepts, principles, and skills you are learning. The lists may include specific tasks or steps you could undertake, the problems and opportunities you might encounter, and—noted in a column alongside those lists—the names of people who might help or hinder you in your efforts.*

* These last two paragraphs are based on my consultation with Dr. Diane Goldsmith, who directs continuing business education programs for The Wharton School, University of Pennsylvania.

■ Preparing a Research Paper

To meet the due date, schedule on your calendar when you will *start* each of the following major steps by counting back from the date your paper is due and estimating approximately how many days you should allow for each step. Until you are experienced in preparing research papers, shorten the time for each major step by seeking help from a university writing center or a professional writing consultant. Even if you are somewhat experienced, you may benefit from consulting a book or article about ways to do advanced writing in a particular discipline.

■ Research

1. Choose your topic carefully.
   a) Jot down as many topics as you can think of related to a subject that is appropriate or actually assigned for your paper.
   b) Evaluate the topics you've listed, considering especially your genuine personal interest in each topic and its likely value for you.
   c) Limit and organize your topic both before and during your research on it. To decide what to include, consider what you know and want to know about the topic, what the instructor has assigned, and how much time you have to complete the paper.
      1) Build your paper around a question, for which the paper serves as a well-balanced and well-organized answer, with all the necessary evidence to support your points.

2) Or, develop and defend a potent idea or thesis about the subject with explicit reference to alternative views and possibilities, which you should research carefully and present fairly.

2. Write a list of as many questions as you can think of about your topic. Study the questions to:
   a) find possible categories that might be included in your paper;
   b) eliminate questions that are likely to take you too far from your central topic.

> Build your paper around a question . . . or develop and defend a potent idea or thesis about the subject.

3. Get an overview of your topic by reading a general source, such as an encyclopedia article, and note names, events, terms, or ideas that you might use in your library search for specific sources.

4. Locate and note information sources efficiently.
   a) Take advantage of the information sheets on library use and services that are available in your library. Use the library's printed guides and take a tour to learn how the library is organized and whether there are any special collections or departmental libraries in your subject area.
   b) Revise your list of subject headings or key words to use in researching your topic. Ask the reference librarians for advice at this stage; they can suggest headings to use as well as sources to consult.
   c) Locate appropriate books through the library's catalog. This may be a card catalog, an on-line (computerized) catalog, or a combination of both.
      1) From the catalog, note on separate notepad pages the author, title, location, and call number of all books that seem likely to contain useful in-

formation. In making your choices, notice the date of publication and the scope and tone indicated by the title.

2) Find and look over each promising book to determine further its possible usefulness. Check the table of contents and the index, the qualifications of the author, and the degree of scholarship that the author demonstrates in writing about an aspect of the subject you know something about.

3) Indicate in an upper corner of the bibliographical slip the status of the book, e.g., "not in the library," "not useful," "being called in," or other information, and group the slips accordingly.

d) Check the periodical indexes in the reference room for current journal, magazine, and newspaper articles on your subject. This is another point at which a reference librarian can help you plan your work. Most libraries offer computerized literature searching. There may be a fee for this service, but it can often provide an extensive list of references on your subject and save you a great amount of time.

e) Write a full bibliographical card* only for those books and periodicals from or about which you expect to take notes. Use standard bibliographical form, as discussed below.

f) If important materials on your topic are not accessible, *consider changing your topic.*

5. Read portions of the books appropriate to the subject and make page notations and notes of your ideas about the material.

a) As you read, note the pages and parts of pages (A, B, C, D, E) from which you think you'll want to take notes when you complete most of your reading; make these notations on the bibliographical card for the book (see pages 18–19).

b) Note on separate cards each of your own original ideas regarding the subject, indicating the author and page number of the material about which you are commenting.

6. Ordinarily, do *not* take notes *yet* from the content itself. *Arrange for a conference with your professor* when you have read enough to know one or two theses or questions that seem promising bases for your paper. You can save immeasurable time and effort and insure the success of your paper if you discuss your plans at this point with your professor or supervisor. During the discussion, take careful notes of any recommendations.

7. Write a tentative and very brief outline, drawing from your note cards.

8. Take notes from your reading.

a) Return to the pages you've noted and, if the material still seems valuable in view of the thesis you have decided upon, take notes of some kind: summaries, quotations, paraphrasing.

b) Use a separate card for each new idea. Note the subject in the upper right-hand corner and the au-

---

* *Books:* Author, title, edition, place of publication, publisher, date of publication. *Articles:* Author, article title, periodical title, volume, date, pages.

thor's name and the exact page reference in the upper left-hand corner.

c) Take great care to avoid plagiarism and infringement of copyright. For any and every source you use in your paper, note the reference for your quotation or paraphrase, in a footnote or parentheses as recommended by your instructor or a style manual. For well-illustrated guidance in avoiding plagiarism, see *A Handbook for Writers*, 4th ed., by Wilfred Stone and J. G. Bell (New York: McGraw-Hill, 1983). For detailed guidance in avoiding copyright infringement, see a library or legal reference book, such as *Henn on Copyright Law: A Practitioner's Guide*, 3rd ed., by Harry G. Henn (New York: Practising Law Institute, 1991), brief excerpts of which are provided in the appendix of this book.

9. It is very important that you add to your notes your critical appraisal and original ideas about the material, noting the author and the page number of the material you are commenting about.

10. Use your ingenuity to discover other possible sources of information in addition to books and periodicals: for example, find individuals who are informed on the subject and draw from your personal experience.

11. Compile clear definitions of all important terms.

12. Keep notepad pages or index cards handy for noting ideas that may come to you in odd moments and add these to your collection of notes.

■ Write

1. First of all, use a word processor if at all possible. They are invaluable aids to efficient and effective thinking and writing.

2. Prepare a brief statement of the thesis, purpose, and/or scope of your paper to serve as a point of reference to keep you close to your subject as you write.

3. Write a full outline, following the steps below:
   a) Arrange your notes carefully in what seems to be an appropriate sequence.

      b) Include definitions of key terms.

      c) Add cards with notes of any new ideas, insights, and conclusions that come to you as you review all the notes that you have taken from your readings.

      d) From your note cards, write your outline in sentence form, to insure clarity and continuity as you write your paper from it.

4. Write a first draft of your paper.

      a) Review comments by professors or supervisors on your previous papers for ideas that can improve your current paper.

      b) Write point by point from your outline, reorganizing when it seems desirable; write the introduction later if it seems difficult to express at first.

      c) In footnotes or endnotes, give credit to (cite) all the sources of ideas and quotations not your own. (See 8c under "Research" on page 72.)

      d) Consult a current standard style manual for an appropriate and consistent form for footnotes and bibliography; for example, the *MLA Handbook*, *Manual for Biological Journals*, or *American Psychological Association Publications Manual*. (See Bibliography.) If you are not sure, ask your instructor which style manual to use.

      e) Strive for fluent expression, not precise diction, in the first draft; bracket words that you think should be replaced in later drafts.

      f) Develop a strong introduction and conclusion. The introduction should state your thesis or question clearly; the conclusion should include a brief summary and restatement of the thesis or question.

■ Revise

1. After completing your first draft and making a printout if you are using a word processor, wait at least a day to allow time for mental refreshment. Then reread and polish the draft.

      a) Check: Are your points clear? Does every paragraph develop the thesis? Is the progression logical and coherent? Could a person reading your paper for the first time preview it easily? Make the changes necessary for you to answer yes to all these questions.

b) Find the precise words to express your points.

c) Reread parts of the paper aloud to reveal any rough spots.

d) In a long paper, provide additional organizational aids for the reader (for example, a table of contents and headings).

2. Write a second draft of the pages that need major revision and allow time for mental refreshment again. (Several revisions may be desirable, if time is available.)

3. Type or print out a final draft. Proofread and correct it. Print a final copy if you are using a word processor.

4. Be sure to print a spare, make a copy by carbon, or photocopy the paper for your own safekeeping.

■ Submit

Turn the paper in on time (or, if absolutely necessary, arrange for a new deadline that is possible for you to meet and acceptable to your professor or supervisor).

■ Using Four Methods for Effective Study and Analogous Activities

Many of the preceding sections of this book referred to four basic and interdependent methods of improving reading, writing, and study: previewing, selecting, chunking, and deep processing.

The four methods can be used for lengthy as well as brief activities: for taking around-the-world trips and writing dissertations or preparing for comprehensive examinations, as well as for taking short trips and studying single chapters. For an extended study task, previewing involves determining carefully the scope of the task. Selecting and chunking involve dividing the whole into parts, deciding which tasks to work on first and which to work on most thoroughly, then grouping the tasks that can be done best in close relationship. Deep processing involves studying one chunk after another, using the ways of thinking about the material that are most appropriate for each chunk and for your purposes.

Naturally, previewing, selecting, chunking, and deep processing are not always necessary or desirable. They *are* necessary and desirable when efficiency is important and when the major purpose is accomplishment of some kind within limited time and in a competitive situation—the conditions of most academic work. For other activities, just one or two of the methods might be desirable or useful. For instance, when you're on vacation you may enjoy simply wandering, without studying a map of the area, and when you come upon a shelf of books you may enjoy simply choosing a book on whim and wandering through it.

Here is a graphic summary of the *Four Methods Basic to Effective Study*:

Four Methods Basic to Effective Study

Preview
Preview books that you need to study for an exam or to write a research paper.

Select
Select the book most interesting or appropriate to start with, preferably one providing an overview of the subject.

Chunk
Chunk by grouping the books according to subject, author, or other aspect related to your purposes.

Process
Process the book in ways most appropriate for your purposes, such as outlining answers to anticipated exam questions or making notes for a research paper.

Preview
Preview the chapter most interesting to you or most appropriate for your purposes.

Select
Select the part of the chapter most interesting or appropriate to read first.

Chunk
Chunk by grouping parts of the chapter according to problems to be solved or questions to be answered or according to sections appropriate for note taking. Read one chunk at a time.

Process
After reading a chunk, process in ways most appropriate for your purposes: reciting what you have learned or solving a problem or answering a question, or noting ideas about the material and pages and parts of pages from which to take notes of the content eventually.

■ Developing a Habit or Hobby of Strengthening Vocabulary

1. When reading or listening, write every unfamiliar word on an index card.
   a) Note the phrase in which you found the word (or the page and part of page—indicated by A, B̄, C, D, E—noting the phrase later).
   b) Guess the meaning from the context of the word and from structural clues, but do not write down your guess. Read on.
2. After collecting a number of words, add to each index card, using a good dictionary,* the following information:
   a) any part of the pronunciation you're not sure about;
   b) phrase in which you found the word (with quotation marks);
   c) derivation, if it will help you remember the meaning;
   d) meaning that is appropriate for the context quoted;
   e) other useful meanings, synonyms, and antonyms;
   f) definitions of unfamiliar synonyms or antonyms (to clarify any subtle differences between these and the key word);

---

* For studying in your major field or at a level above that of an introductory course in a discipline new to you, you should own a current, authoritative dictionary specific to the field; for example, in literature, William Harmon and C. Hugh Holman's *Handbook to Literature* (New York: MacMillan, 1986).

g) other forms of the word such as in other parts of speech, or in idioms;

h) word on the back of the card for drill purposes.

3. Study new words in odd moments, thinking of ways you might use them in actual contexts. For each word:

a) study the spelling, definition, and any other information you have noted about the word;

> Study new words in odd moments, thinking of ways you might use them in actual contexts.

b) write the word from memory; check immediately for accuracy;

c) recite the definition and other information from memory; check immediately for accuracy.

Here are two examples of vocabulary cards that I have accumulated since I began the hobby of word collecting years ago. I include them here to illustrate that note taking on words can be very brief, including only information that will help you understand, remember, and want to use the word.

euphoric

"The experience [Harvard] tends to be more astringent than *euphoric*"

From Greek "eu" = well
        + "phoric" = to bear
"giving a sense of well-being and buoyancy; incapable of depression or readily shaking it."

heuristic
- "start with it as a heuristic principle"
- "the use of the heuristic hunch"

From Greek, "to discover" — EUREKA!

"serving to find out (for oneself), such as an educational system in which student is trained to find out things for self."

◼ Learning a Foreign Language

In learning a foreign language, you can apply or adapt many of the ideas in the preceding sections, beginning with "Remembering Effectively" (pages 10–11) "Mastering textbook material" (pages 24–28), and "Developing a Habit or Hobby of Strengthening Vocabulary" (pages 77–79). Other sections of this book can help you read, write, and study in a foreign language as well as in your native language.

However, learning a foreign language requires additional methods and effort:

1. Use audiotapes regularly; these accompany most textbooks for foreign-language study.
2. Study frequently—six days a week—in short, intensive sessions.
3. In learning new words, cluster or group about five words that are related in some way; then study the words one cluster at a time.
4. Study most intensively the words and phrases that you find most difficult to remember.
   a) Use as many senses, in as many ways as you can, while thinking. For example, write the word or phrase while looking at it and saying it, think about its parts and its meaning, write it again while saying it but not looking at it, check to see if you got it right. Repeat this process several times.
   b) Look for some way to relate the difficult word to something familiar and think of this relationship as you continue to rehearse the word.
   c) Write the word or phrase on index cards, as de-

scribed in "Strengthening vocabulary," and review the cards orally several times a day in odd moments and before you go to sleep the night before a test.

5. Read passages for their general meaning, without concern for recognizing every word. When you encounter an unfamiliar word, write it on a 3-by-5-inch memo page or index card. When you have finished reading the passage, decide which words you need to learn, and proceed to learn them by following the method described above.

6. Look for opportunities to use the foreign language in real-life situations or with other students of the language. Use it for greetings and for expressing ideas and thoughts that are important to you. Rehearse for real-life use by imagining situations that involve several speakers and playing all the roles. Read current foreign-language newspapers and magazines and see

foreign-language films. Learn songs in the language and sing them aloud. Try to visit places where the language is spoken widely. Such real-life use can enhance your motivation and increase your learning in ways no other method can.

> Look for opportunities to use the foreign language in real-life situations.

If you have severe problems mastering a foreign language, you might need special help. Usually this involves more repetition and more time to learn the language. Seek help through your instructor, the faculty member responsible for language instruction in your school, a learning center, and/or an office for students who are disabled (including learning disabled).

■ Improving Writing

If you look back in this book, you will see that there is only one section, "Preparing a Research Paper," that is specifically about writing. The rest of the sections are more directly about reading. But reading and writing, speaking and listening, are so closely related that some of the ways to improve each can also be applied to improving the others.

The relationships between reading and writing and the ways to improve them can be made clearer by using the same terms for their similar aspects. For example, we could say that in reading expository writing we look for a thesis statement and ways by which it is supported, while in writing we develop a thesis statement and ways to support it. Similarly, we could use the terms *previewing*, *selecting*, *chunking*, and *deep processing*, which are described on pages 75–76 as ways to improve reading, in describing ways to improve writing.

Here, then, are direct suggestions for ways you can improve your writing, in terms of the ways recommended for improving reading. In writing as in reading, the activities are interrelated or overlap. While reading is like eating a dinner, writing is like creating a dinner. It usually involves some step-by-step activities, but mostly it involves back-and-forth considering and doing, reconsidering and revising, until just before the guests sit down to eat.

■ Prepare to write

1. Collect as much material as you can about your subject before you try to write a first draft. For a research paper, this should involve the kind of reading and note

taking described in "Preparing a Research Paper" (pages 68–74).

2. Make notes of your ideas and observations. To save time, write each idea or observation on separate small pages or cards, so that you can arrange and rearrange them before you write your first draft.

■ Preview

Previewing is helpful at several times during the writing process but especially after you've collected as much material as you can and before you write your first draft.

1. Preview all the notes that you have accumulated on your subject.
2. If the genre in which you are to write is unfamiliar to you, ask your instructor, a librarian, or another authority to recommend a model of the genre to examine so that you can get a good sense of the structure of it.
3. At some point as you were preparing to write, you may have developed a question or idea about the subject which guided you as you made notes; if not, you should try to think of such a question or idea as you preview. At the same time, look for relationships among the ideas you have collected that might contribute to answering your question or supporting your idea or thesis.

■ Select and chunk

Sort and group your notes according to the relationships you see as you preview:

1. *Select* by deciding on a question or thesis and the most promising way to answer the question or support the thesis.
2. Select the audience for which you want to write and keep that audience in mind as you write and revise, to make what you say and how you say it as appropriate as possible. In an academic situation, the audience is mainly the instructor; keep your particular instructor in mind.

3. Select from your notes all those that are appropriate for the question or thesis and the audience you have selected.

4. *Chunk* by sketching a pattern—a map or an outline—to represent your decisions about how you will group and arrange your ideas.

5. Write your outline in full sentences. These sentences should be the main assertions that you feel ready to make in answer to your question or in support of your thesis. Keep in mind that you may change these assertions as you continue to write.

■ Process deeply

1. Write your paper following your map or outline and your notes. Feel free to reconceive and reorder your ideas as you see new relationships or even discover a better question or a more potent thesis.

2. Support your points with carefully chosen examples or clarify them through analogies or metaphors (implied analogies).

3. You will have processed deeply in preparing to write and in previewing, selecting, and chunking. You will be continuing to process deeply as you write, as you revise your paper, and when at last you read your finished product. Because deep processing occurs throughout the writing process, writing is regarded as a way of knowing or getting to know, not just a way of telling.

> Writing is regarded as a way of knowing . . . not just a way of telling.

4. Revise your draft and rewrite until you feel satisfied enough with your product to show it to a friend.

5. Ask your friend to respond to a particular part of your writing that you are concerned about. Revise your

writing in the light of any of the friend's suggestions that seem right to you.

6. In some schools or departments or classes, this sort of sharing of papers may not be appropriate or acceptable. When this is the case, allow several days between each rereading of your drafts and read them as if you were the audience for whom you have written.

7. Examine each draft for ways to make it more easily previewable by your readers and clearer and more readable in style.

8. Edit your final draft; weed out redundancies, imprecisions, and errors in grammar or spelling. Realize that you will find ways to improve your paper whenever you reread it; it will never be perfect—and it need not be. Just do your best in the time you have.

To illustrate the process I have recommended, I will describe how I wrote these pages.

To prepare to write them, I noted on 3-by-5-inch memo pages all the ideas that came to my mind about ways to write more effectively, particularly for academic or professional purposes. I read or reviewed half a dozen books about writing, noting pages and parts of pages from which I might want to take notes eventually. As I read, I noted my own new ideas about my subject immediately, each idea on a separate memo page.

When I felt I had done enough reading or reviewing for my purposes, I returned to my notations of pages and parts of pages and made notes from each book on separate 3-by-5-inch pages, noting the author and page number in the upper left corner.

When I felt I had accumulated enough notes and ideas, I previewed all my notes, looking for relationships among them and ways that they might best be arranged to answer the question, "What suggestions should I give to students for improving the way they go about their writing?" As I previewed, I wrote additional notes when new ideas occurred to me. I also began to sort the note pages into stacks and jotted down headings for each stack. Here are the headings I jotted down:

> *Reading related to writing*
> *Previewing*
> *Selecting*
> *Chunking*
> *Deep processing*
> *Books about improving writing*

Then I wrote a first draft of the assertions I felt I could make and ways that I might support the assertions. Here is what I wrote:

> *As reading and writing are related, so are ways to improve them.*
> *Previewing, selecting, chunking, and deep processing can be applied to writing as well as to reading.*
> *Explain application.*
> *Illustrate.*
> *Read books about improving writing.*

Following this rough outline and my matching stacks of notes, I wrote a first draft. I set the draft aside for about a week. When I reread the draft I marked revisions directly on it. A week later I copied the revised draft, editing as I typed.

I read the draft aloud to myself and made more changes. I duplicated the revised second draft so that I could show it to one of my colleagues, Susan L. Lytle. She suggested that I revise the pages to build up the part about preparing to write, make more statements about improving writing, and weed out some of the details of my explanations. She also suggested that I illustrate the process I was recommending by using some other writing than the pages themselves. I followed the first three suggestions, but I decided not to follow the last one.

In my first draft I realized, to my surprise, that I had forgotten my main audience. I was writing for teachers, who are the audience for most of my professional writing, rather than students. When I wrote the second draft I kept in mind an audience of students or a particular student. I also kept in mind the structure and metaphors I had used for the earlier draft. I typed a third draft of the pages, edited it briefly, and read it aloud to myself. I made additional changes indicated by the way the words sounded when I read them aloud.

I duplicated the third draft to show to several more of my colleagues. They pointed out sentences that I could make clearer or more concise.

I typed a fourth draft and sent this to my editor, Bob Boynton. Bob suggested that I be more realistic or frank in making some of my points; for example, I should admit that the only audience for most student writing "is the teacher, unfortunately."

The result of the process I have just described is the section that you are reading now.

Learning to use a word processor, which I did between the second and third editions of this book, has enhanced my writing. Using it saves immeasurable time and makes the writing process so much more pleasurable and the product so much more readable that it actually helps prevent procrastination and increase concentration.

Buy or rent a word processor if you can, or arrange to use one regularly through the computer resource center at your school, office, or copy store.

For more ideas about ways to improve your writing, look for books on the subject in libraries or bookstores, especially college bookstores on the shelves labeled for English composition courses, and consult teachers of writing for their recommendations.

Here are some books about improving writing that are recommended highly:

Belanoff, Pat, et al. *The Right Handbook*. Portsmouth, NH: Heinemann-Boynton/Cook, 1986.

Berthoff, Ann E., with James Stephens. *Forming/Thinking/Writing*. 2nd ed. Portsmouth, NH: Heinemann-Boynton/Cook, 1988.

Brannon, Lil, et al. *Writers Writing*. Portsmouth, NH: Heinemann-Boynton/Cook, 1982.

Elbow, Peter. *Writing Without Teachers*. New York: Oxford University Press, 1973.

Flower, Linda. *Problem Solving Strategies for Writing*. 3rd ed. San Diego: Harcourt, 1989.

Kaye, Sanford. *Writing Under Pressure: The Quick Writing Process*. New York: Oxford University Press, 1989.

Macrorie, Ken. *The I-Search Paper*. Portsmouth, NH: Heinemann-Boynton/Cook, 1988.

Murray, Donald M. *Expecting the Unexpected: Teaching Myself—and Others—to Read and Write*. Portsmouth, NH: Heinemann-Boynton/Cook, 1989.

Schwartz, Mimi. *Writing for Many Roles*. Portsmouth, NH: Heinemann-Boynton/Cook, 1985.

Stone, Wilfred, and J. G. Bell. *Prose Style: A Handbook for Writers*. 4th ed. New York: McGraw-Hill, 1983.

Williams, Joseph. *Style: Ten Lessons in Clarity and Grace*. 3rd ed. Glenview, IL: Scott Foresman, 1988.

∎ Preparing for Examinations

The best preparation for examinations is regular study, including reviewing and learning class notes after every lecture or two, mastering each textbook assignment on first reading it, and using other study strategies described in earlier sections of this book.

Special review, beginning at least a few days before the exam, is also necessary. The general recommendations in "Remembering Effectively" (pages 10–11) support the detailed procedures listed below.

The best preparation for examinations is regular study.

1. Plan a realistic study schedule and stick to it as closely as possible.
   a) Decide how much material you must review and approximately how long one unit of it will take; divide the number of units over the time available and note this on your calendar.
   b) Distribute your study time over at least two ses-

sions for minor tests and at least four for major exams. Review periods should be relatively brief, because recalling and organizing ideas is so fatiguing that efficiency usually decreases rapidly after about an hour of review.

2. If a problem or plan in another area of your life is distracting, keep paper handy for noting ideas or feelings that occur to you about the problem or plan; wait until a study break to think more about them. (See the section "Improving Concentration, Motivation, and Willpower," pages 107–111.)

3. Study *actively*.

   a) Begin by quickly previewing all your class notes and making a one-page outline (a table of contents) for them.

   b) Study as a unit each subject within the course, for example, all your notes from all sources on the same subject.

      1) Treat your class notes as you would treat a textbook chapter. After reviewing your table of contents, review and recite one section (one chunk) at a time.

      2) Review your one-page outline for each textbook chapter and then recite or write briefly from memory; reread portions of the textbook *only* if you can't remember the supporting details well; they should come to your mind as you encounter each cue on your outline.

      3) Prepare and study a master outline of important aspects of the subject for which lectures, textbooks, and supplementary reading interrelate.

> Create graphic aids to help you understand and remember the material: for example, a time line, an outline map, a model of a theory.

c) Create graphic aids to help you understand and remember the material: for example, a time line, an
outline map, a model of a theory.

d) While reading and reviewing, build a list of page
and part-of-page references (A, B, C, D, E) about
major terms or concepts. In reviewing for exams,
take notes from these page references on separate
notepad pages. Arrange the pages for each term or
concept in an order that will help you develop a
clear and comprehensive definition.

e) Build a list of terms, using indentation to show relationships among them. Fold the list in half length-
wise; think about the definition of each term; for
definitions you find hard to remember, write the definitions briefly on the right-hand side of the list.

f) Avoid artificial (that is, insignificant) mnemonic
(memory) devices, because these cannot help you
understand the material. Instead, group key terms
or ideas in significant ways. See examples of both
significant and insignificant mnemonic devices on
pages 95–97.

g) Review the notes you made during your regular
study, in answer to critical and creative questions
like those recommended on pages 59–61, and write

down any questions or ideas that come to your mind about the material you are reviewing.

   1) In particular, use your imagination and your knowledge of controversies in the field you are studying to change the point of view from which you think about the subject.

   2) Make notes of your new insights.

h) For an essay exam, make up exam questions or ask your professor if old exam questions are available and think through or roughly outline your answers to the questions. (Do this no later than two days before the exam.)

   1) Anticipate one or two very broad questions that the instructor might ask. As you review your notes, write down points and pages appropriate for an answer to the question(s).

   2) Cooperate with a friend in making up and exchanging more limited (and more likely) exam questions; in a dress-rehearsal situation, outline your answers to the friend's questions; later, discuss your answers with your friend.

   3) Build a structure by which to recall key ideas that you are likely to need quickly—for example,

the elements to consider in analyzing a poem or a painting, or the factors to consider in analyzing a problem in economics.

i) Pretend to teach—or actually arrange to tutor—portions of the subject on which you will be examined. Tutoring usually results in the teacher learning more than the student (some of the probable reasons may be found in the section "Remembering Effectively," pages 10–11).

4. Allow time to pay special attention to the parts of the material that you have found hardest.

a) Testing yourself will help you find your weak spots; work on these most.

b) Just before going to sleep on the night before the exam, review the hardest parts, your master outlines, and your outlines of answers to the questions that you or your friend have anticipated.

5. Get ample sleep two nights before the exam (in case you have any problem sleeping the next night), as well as the night before the exam (so that you can remember and think as clearly as possible while taking the exam). Rest assured that you will be expected to have thought critically and creatively about the subject matter of the course before you take the examination. Having thought and rested, you will feel more confident in facing an essay exam that includes questions like "Shakespeare and the common people. Discuss." or "The French Revolution. Who won?"

Talking over the things which you have read with your companions on the first proper opportunity you have for it, is a most useful manner of review or repetition, in order to fix them upon the mind. Teach them to your younger friends, in order to establish your own knowledge while you communicate it to them. The animal powers of your tongue and of your ear, as well as your intellectual faculties, will all join together to help the memory. Hermetus studied hard in a remote corner of the land, and in solitude, yet he be-

came a very learned man. He seldom was so happy as to enjoy suitable society at home, and therefore he talked over to the fields and the woods in the evening what he had been reading in the day. . . .

ISAAC WATTS (1741)

■ An example of grouping ideas in significant ways

Imagine that you have to learn in detail the psychology of Abraham Maslow and that you are studying the graphic aid in *The Third Force: The Psychology of Abraham Maslow** reprinted here. To remember the sixteen "growth needs," you should look for a basis of clustering or grouping the terms that is consistent with Maslow's psychology. You should avoid grouping on insignificant bases such as alphabetizing, common suffixes, or forming a sentence from words that begin with the first letter of each of the growth needs.

How might you cluster or group the growth needs then? Realizing that, according to Maslow's theories, growth needs are

1. nonhierarchical (that is, with no particular order of precedence)
2. derived from Maslow's study of individuals who seem to have achieved "self-actualization"

you could group the growth needs in fours according to your own conception of related needs or characteristics and then think of someone you know who seems to exemplify each of the four groups.

To recall the growth needs, you would then simply recall the four individuals you know who exemplify the characteristics; by association, you would remember the groups of related terms (needs/characteristics) that you have identified with the four individuals. By studying this way, you would not only remember the sixteen growth needs but also better understand the psychological theory of Abraham Maslow.

---

*Frank Goble, *The Third Force: The Psychology of Abraham Maslow*, p. 52. Copyright © 1970 by Thomas Jefferson Research Center. Reprinted by permission of Viking Penguin, a division of Penguin Books USA, Inc.

Abraham Maslow's Hierarchy of Needs

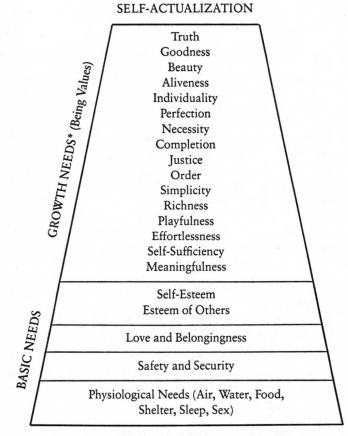

SELF-ACTUALIZATION

GROWTH NEEDS* (Being Values)

Truth
Goodness
Beauty
Aliveness
Individuality
Perfection
Necessity
Completion
Justice
Order
Simplicity
Richness
Playfulness
Effortlessness
Self-Sufficiency
Meaningfulness

Self-Esteem
Esteem of Others

Love and Belongingness

Safety and Security

Physiological Needs (Air, Water, Food, Shelter, Sleep, Sex)

BASIC NEEDS

The External Environment
Preconditions for Need Satisfaction:
Freedom, Justice, Orderliness,
Challenge (Stimulation)

---

*Growth needs are all of equal importance (not hierarchical).

(1)	(2)	(3)	(4)
Truth	Aliveness	Necessity	Completion
Goodness	Individuality	Justice	Simplicity
Beauty	Richness	Order	Effortlessness
Perfection	Playfulness	Self-sufficiency	Meaningfulness

Exemplified by

1) _____ 2) _____ 3) _____ 4) _____

*W*hatsoever you would trust to your memory let it be disposed in a proper method, connected well together, and referred to distinct and particular heads or classes both general and particular.

ISAAC WATTS (1741)

■ Taking Examinations

■ Essay examinations

1. Prepare to begin: Take several slow, deep breaths through your nose. Check the time and ask whether it will be announced at all during the exam.
2. Underline key words in the directions and questions to focus your thinking, help you keep calm, and prevent you from trying to write before you are settled and organized.
3. Read through all of the questions; jot down a few words that come to mind about each question you plan to answer (if there is a choice).

> Read through all of the questions; jot down a few words that come to mind about each question you plan to answer.

4. Budget your time.
   a) Consider the number of points given for each question, if this information is stated.
   b) Decide how much time you should allot for each answer, considering your knowledge of the subject and the number of points given.
   c) Allow time for a rough outline before writing each answer and for proofreading after completing the exam.
5. As a rule, answer the easiest question (or second eas-

iest) first, to increase your confidence and give you more time to recall answers for the harder questions.

6. Jot down a rough outline from which to write your answer for each question.

   a) In a column, write key words and phrases related to points that you remember from lectures and from your reading and thinking for the course.

   b) Then think *beyond* these first ideas to new ideas that occur to you in response to the question; these ideas may be based upon your own experiences and interests as well as the lectures and readings for the course.

   c) Number your ideas in the most appropriate order for your answer.

   d) If you run out of time in answering the question, copy the ideas from your outline to complete your answer briefly.

7. Take care to answer precisely the question asked.

   a) Notice especially the limitation stressed by the instruction verb (list, analyze, compare).

   b) Form the first sentence by turning the question into a statement or by writing a thesis sentence that you will support with specific examples or evidence.

   c) Include a time frame, indicating, for example, whether a historical movement extended over decades or centuries.

   d) When in doubt, qualify your answers by using approximate times or dates and by including qualifying words (for example, "some," "most," "usually," or "occasionally") in your statements.

   e) Underline the key phrases in your answer, so that the hurried exam reader will not miss a single one of them.

8. Begin a new paragraph for each point on your outline.

9. Support your main points with carefully chosen evidence or examples.

10. Abbreviate long names or terms that you will need to repeat frequently and include a code at the top of the page on which you first use the abbreviation (for example, T = Tchaikovsky; R = Revolution).

11. Write clearly, concisely, and legibly. (If you prefer to

type, inquire in advance about the possibility of typing your exam.)

12. Leave a space after each paragraph to allow for possible additions when you proofread; or write your answers only on the front side of each page so that you can insert additions on the back of the preceding page.

Support your main points with carefully chosen evidence or examples.

13. Proofread your answer.
14. After you take an exam and it is returned to you, use it to determine how to study for and take exams more successfully.

■ Sample essay question

If you were given an examination on the material in this book, an appropriate question might be this one:

What advice would you give a friend who asks you for help with a serious problem—the tendency to panic at exam time?

On a separate piece of paper, follow steps 6 through 13 for taking essay examinations; then compare what you have written with the sample essay illustrated here in longhand.

Question rephrased in opening statement.

If a friend asked me for advice about his problem of panicking at exam time, this is what I would tell him.

Question interpreted broadly.

Consider yourself <u>preparing for exams from the first day of class</u>. Learn each chunk of new material as you encounter it; for example, learn lecture notes within 24 hours after every class. Preview all nonfiction material recommended and read it selectively; delay taking notes about the content (noting instead pages and parts of pages to which you may return for note taking), but note immediately your own ideas about the material. Preview required textbook chapters, and prepare a one-page outline of each chapter as you read it.

Space left between paragraphs.

<u>Plan a special review</u> several days before the exam. Begin by building a table of contents for your class notes. Plan your study time by estimating how much time you'll need to review one chunk and multiplying by the number of chunks you have.

Write on your calendar when you should study each chunk, counting back from the date the exam is scheduled. Study actively; for example, create graphic aids and formulate answers to anticipated exam questions as you study. Two nights (at least) before the exam, exchange anticipated questions with a friend and outline your answers to unfamiliar questions; in this way you'll be having almost a dress rehearsal of the exam. The night before the exam, get enough sleep so that you will feel as alert and able to cope as possible.

> Main points underlined.

Take precautions in taking the exam. Underline key words in the directions and in the questions to calm your nerves and keep you from starting to write before you're ready. Budget your time, allowing first for a rough outline of your answer and last for proofreading. Skip lines after each paragraph to allow space for inserting any new ideas you think of during proofreading.

Take advantage of professional counseling or University Counseling Service workshops to overcome test anxiety. For this to be most effective, do it at least two months before your exams.

Briefly then, overcoming panic at exam time is likely to require regular study from the very beginning of the course, special preparation several days in advance of the exam, precautions while taking the exam, and perhaps—for best results—the help of a counseling psychologist.

> Main points summarized—including an aspect of
> this essay that goes beyond the recommendations
> given in this booklet. (See 6b on page 99.)

■ Objective examinations

The brief suggestions and examples below are for taking verbal aptitude tests. For more extensive suggestions for taking objective tests, see *How to Take Tests*, by Jason Millman and Walter Pauk (New York: McGraw-Hill, 1969). For help in taking objective examinations in the health sciences, look for books like *Test-Taking Skills in Dentistry*, by Randolph E. Sarnacki (Philadelphia: Lea and Ferbinger, 1982).

The Graduate Record Examinations® (GRE®) "Registration and Information Bulletin," like many other test information bulletins, includes clear and detailed directions for taking graduate school tests, as well as sample questions with answers. Test information bulletins may also recommend strategies for answering different types of questions. However, the strategies are not always efficient, even though they are effective.

The recommendations below are meant to supplement suggestions in bulletins like the GRE® "Registration and Information Bulletin." For test takers who are concerned about completing a test within its time limits, the strategies described here are efficient as well as effective ways to answer several types of questions. Try these strategies, as well as those offered in official bulletins and in commercial materials for standardized tests. Choose the ones that seem to work best for you and practice them until you feel confident and competent enough to do your best on the test for which you are preparing.

The examples offered below are from the GRE® "Registration and Bulletin" (Princeton, NJ: Educational Testing Service), 1991–1992. Reprinted by permission.

You can obtain a current edition of the bulletin from: Graduate Record Examinations, Educational Testing Service, Box 6000, Princeton, NJ 08541–6000.

Word opposites

1. When you take a multiple-choice test that requires choosing word opposites, or antonyms, keep in mind that it takes less time to choose words that are alike, or synonyms. Think of the given word as changed to its opposite—by adding "not" to a positive word or by

cutting the "un-" or "in-" negative prefix from a negative word. Then search among the choices for a word that means the *same* as the word(s) now in your mind. For example, change "laborious" to "not laborious," and you will recognize immediately that "easy" is the best answer.

2. If the given word is only slightly familiar to you, but at least you know whether it has a "good" or "bad" connotation, it is probably worth the time to try to answer the question.

3. However, if the given word is totally unfamiliar to you, if you cannot guess even its connotation by examining its root or thinking of words similar in form or sound to it, and if you can't eliminate even one choice as definitely wrong, move on to the next question rather than waste time trying to think of the answer.

Try out the above suggestions on this example:

REFUTABLE: (A) understandable (B) unavoidable (C) indispensable (D) inexpressible (E) indisputable

Analogies

1. Before reading any of the choices given, decide at least two ways in which the key words are related. For example, "torch: liberty": 1) a torch is a symbol of liberty, and 2) a torch is held by the Statue of Liberty.

2. Remember that analogous relationships are usually one of the following kinds:
   a) Part to whole ("spring: watch")
   b) Degree ("hard: formidable")
   c) Cause and effect ("puncture: blowout")
   d) Chronology ("tadpole: frog")
   e) Symbol to symbolized ("torch: liberty")

3. In reading the choices, first consider the words corresponding to just *one* of the two words in the given analogy; then eliminate at least three of the choices given. Next, read the other word in the remaining two choices and decide which choice is better as a final answer. This is a faster method than if you consider *both* words in all of the choices given.

Try out the above suggestions on this example:

EPILOGUE: NOVEL::   (A) lyric: poem
(B) violin: sonata   (C) title: sermon   (D) song: cycle
(E) coda: symphony

Sentence completions

1. Read the whole sentence, with blanks.
2. If there are two blanks, decide from the context what the relationship between the words in the two blanks is likely to be (e.g., are the words likely to be similar or opposite in meaning?); then think about the kind of word that might fit the blank that seems easiest to fill.
3. Read the choices for the one blank only and choose two possible answers from the choices for that blank.
4. Reread the whole sentence twice, filling in the blanks with only the two pairs of answers that you think might be correct. Decide which of the two pairs is better.

   Try out the above suggestions on this example:

The combination of _____ and _____ in Edmund's speech can be startling, especially when he slyly slips in some juicy vulgarity amid the mellifluous circumlocutions of a gentleman of the old school.
(A) tact . . . innocence
(B) raciness . . . ribaldry
(C) piousness . . . modesty
(D) elegance . . . earthiness
(E) propriety . . . bashfulness

Reading comprehension

1. Preview the paragraph(s) by reading:
   a) the first sentence of the first paragraph
   b) the last paragraph
   c) the first and last sentences of any other paragraphs
2. Read the first two questions *without* reading the multiple choices.
3. Read the whole selection with these questions in mind.
4. Read the choices for the first two questions and answer the questions.

5. Use appropriate reading approaches to answer the other questions, for example scan for details, or carefully read a sentence or paragraph in which there is a metaphor that must be explained.

6. To answer questions about inferences or conclusions, select two or three possibilities from the choices. Test each possibility by rereading the paragraph with one inference in mind. When or if a phrase or sentence seems to contradict that inference, stop reading the paragraph and start again with another inference in mind.

Note: In taking multiple-choice tests, keep in mind that statistics show that if you can identify at least one of the choices as wrong, you're fairly safe in guessing the answer; if you can identify at least two of the choices as wrong, you're wise to guess the answer.

In order to discover the value of these procedures and develop the habit of using them, apply them on numerous sample questions given in a reputable book about multiple-choice examinations.

Answers to examples above: E, E, D.

■ Improving Concentration, Motivation, and Willpower

Concentration, motivation, and willpower—attitudes that are essential for the most effective and efficient reading and study—can usually be improved in six basic ways:

1. Look for opportunities to exercise personal choice in your learning activities.

   a) Select courses or study groups on the basis of your genuine interest in the subject and readings and your knowledge about the instructor or leader. To do this, you will need to find out much more than the mere title and brief description of each course and the name of the instructor. You will need to: 1) examine the syllabus (which is usually available in the department office) and the books required and recommended (which are usually available in a particular library or bookstore); 2) ask the opinion of others who have taken part in the same course or group; and 3) visit the first session. Also, visit the first classes or meetings of alternative courses or groups, with the permission of the instructors, so that you can change to one of these if you're not satisfied with your original choice.

   b) If you are starting out in a new school, talk with an academic advisor about choosing courses primarily on the basis that they truly interest you, rather than that they only "get requirements out of the way."

Once you feel successful in your new school, you are likely to study more effectively for any required courses that may be of less interest to you.

c) If possible, select courses that permit you some choice in the books you read and the subjects you write about.

2. Clarify your interests and values in relation to your immediate and long-term goals, personal as well as vocational.

a) Think about your recent choices and what they indicate about your interests and values.

b) Recall times when you have been thoroughly engrossed in what you were reading or writing: What were the elements that may have contributed to your being motivated and able to concentrate? The subject? Instructor? Book? Group? Environment?

c) Discuss your goals with an academic advisor, psychologist at a counseling service, or personnel at a career planning and placement service.

d) Read both fiction and nonfiction that relates to the career and other goals you have been considering.

e) If you have not established a career, seek volunteer or paid experience in the field you have been considering and/or talk at length with individuals who seem to be successful in the field.

3. Study actively and efficiently, using methods like those described in this book; by doing so, you can shorten the time in which you must concentrate, motivate yourself, and use your willpower. In summary:

a) Organize your work and budget your time (see pages 6–9).

b) Increase your background in the subject matter, and so increase your interest in it (see pages 13, 20).

c) Preview before reading expository material, then "chunk" the material; chew and swallow one chunk before biting off another (see pages 6–8, 76).

d) If you tend to procrastinate before or after previewing, start reading at the part of the book or article that you find most interesting (see pages 76, 116).

e) In starting on a research paper, delay taking notes on what a book says, but note your own ideas and questions about it immediately; confirm your plans for the paper with your professor or supervisor before proceeding further (see page 71).

4. Provide for favorable study conditions, like these:
   a) times of day when you feel alert enough to concentrate
   b) adequate light and ventilation
   c) freedom from distractions (for example, noise: if you cannot prevent or move away from distracting noise, set up a closer nondistracting sound, like music without words or a fan, or use medically recommended earplugs)
   d) a seat in which you can be comfortable but also alert

   e) having regular exercise, sufficient and regular sleep, and at least three nourishing (but not heavy) meals a day
   f) recently prescribed glasses, if you need them for reading
   g) freedom from substances that interfere with concentration, such as caffeine, alcohol, and drugs. (Alcohol and drugs are associated with academic failure. If you tend to overuse them, seek help from a psychological, psychiatric, or counseling service.

The sooner you do, the sooner you're likely to be
free of the problem.)

h) occasional study with a carefully chosen group,
with fixed times for starting and ending

5. Keep a memo book or pad handy to note any ideas
that come to your mind that are not directly related to
your study, so that your ideas will be safely on paper,
for later use, instead of on your mind, where they can
distract you.

6. Give attention to possible psychological causes of inadequate concentration, motivation, or willpower.

a) Talk with a psychologist at a university counseling
service or with a psychiatrist at a university mental
health service or in private practice.

b) Read books that can give you insight into your attitudes and behavior. Browse in a bookstore or library, follow up book reviews that appeal to you,
and ask librarians, advisors, psychologists, or ther-
apists for specific recommendations of books and
articles.

*Now in order to gain a greater facility of at-
tention we may observe these rules:*

*1. "Get a good liking to the study or knowledge you
would pursue." We may observe that there is not much
difficulty in confining the mind to contemplate what
we have a great desire to know. . . .*

*2. "Do not choose your constant place of study by
the finery of the prospects, or the most various and entertaining scenes of sensible things." Too much light,
or a variety of objects which strike the eye or the ear,
especially while they are ever in motion or often
changing, have a natural and powerful tendency to
steal away the mind too often from its steady pursuit
of any subject which we contemplate. . . .*

ISAAC WATTS (1741)

The less interested and motivated you feel as to a particular course or reading assignment, the more you should try

to follow the recommendations in this book that are based on principles of learning other than the basic principles of interest and motivation.

As you try just a few of the recommendations, you are likely to experience one small success after another. Each success will increase your confidence and relieve your anxiety—and so improve your concentration, motivation, and willpower.

If you follow the recommendations in this guide and find that you don't progress as much or as rapidly as you had anticipated, arrange for an interview about your reading, writing, and study needs at a university reading/writing improvement service or learning center.

■ Keeping Up in Your Profession: Lifelong Learning

You have graduated from college and perhaps from graduate or professional school, and you are beginning to work in your new job or profession. You know that keeping up with current knowledge in your field and related disciplines is a professional responsibility and that it not only makes you better at what you do, it makes you more interested in it and enthusiastic about it. But how can you work in a demanding profession, keep up with current knowledge in and beyond your immediate areas of responsibility, and also lead a reasonably balanced life? Keeping up is difficult to manage, but it will be easier and take less time if you go about it in an organized way.

When you are working in your field, you will be keeping up with specific aspects related to your immediate responsibilities. To keep up in your field more broadly and efficiently, you will need to use strategies like these, adapting them to your particular profession and style:

1. Through universities, libraries and bookstores, professional organizations, and publishers in your field, find authorities and consult them frequently.
   a) Universities, libraries, and bookstores:
      1) Browse in university and specialized bookstores that stock books for courses in your field and closely related fields. In each book that looks useful, scan the index for topics of particular interest to you, read the table of contents, and pre-

view chapters of immediate interest. This can help you keep up as well as decide what to buy.

2) Examine the syllabi of courses in your field or related fields and choose one or more courses to take or audit.

3) With the help of a reference librarian, make a computerized search for summaries of articles on a subject of your professional interest. Reading the summaries can give you a good overview of information and materials available on the subject and help you decide confidently which materials to locate and read more fully.

4) Examine a "current awareness" publication regularly; for example, *Current Contents* (published by the Institute for Scientific Information, Philadelphia) reprints the tables of contents of current journals in various fields—*Current Contents for Social and Behavioral Sciences, Life Sciences, Arts and Humanities, Engineering, Technology and Applied Science,* and *Physical, Chemical and Earth Sciences.*

5) Clip or photocopy reviews of books that you might want to buy.

b) Professional organizations:

1) Join one or more professional organizations, at least for a year's trial. Some organizations have reduced rates for the first year or for student members.

2) Subscribe to at least one journal published by each organization that you join; attend some of the organizations' seminars, conferences, or conventions; and buy some books and tapes that they make available.

3) If you cannot attend a conference you are interested in, ask the sponsors for a program and occasionally write to speakers requesting copies of their presentation or any materials distributed.

4) Submit articles of your own to journals of the organizations or prepare presentations for their conferences.

c) Publishers:

1) Browse through the catalogs of publishing companies in your field, note books for possible ordering, and request that your name be added to the publishers' mailing lists.

2) Save time and avoid errors in purchasing books by browsing in the publishers' exhibits that are part of many professional conventions and placing orders there for books you have examined.

3) Buy a current dictionary or handbook for your field.

2. Prepare to keep up with your reading by previewing and selecting.

a) When you add a book or journal to your library, or borrow one from a friend in your field or from a library, take a few minutes to prepare to read it. In the table of contents, if the book is your own, make a short line or question mark next to each chapter or article that you think you want to read soon. If you have borrowed the book, photocopy the title page, copyright notice, and table of contents so that you can mark them freely and save them for future reference.

b) As soon as possible, preview sections, chapters, or articles of immediate interest to get a sense of their scope and quality and to satisfy your curiosity temporarily. Make an X by any articles or chapters that you think are not worth reading further.

c) If you want to remember what you previewed, tell

yourself or a companion about it from memory, before moving on.

d) When you expect to travel or have some other appropriate time for reading professional material, take the books or journals that you have previewed and selected.

> Prepare to keep up with your reading by previewing and selecting.

3. Make notes appropriate for your purposes.

a) When you read, make notes according to the sections of this book on "Saving Time in Taking Notes" and "Critical and Creative Reading."

b) Write the notes in any of several places, according to how or where you want to store your notes: at the top of the first page of the article or chapter, on the flyleaf, on index cards, or on 8½-by-11-inch paper. Two of the advantages of making most of your notes on separate cards or pages, rather than in the books or journals themselves, are that the books will be more readable without distracting marks (for you and others who may read them in the future) and that you will still have the notes if you give away, lend, or lose the book.

c) Note a reminder of your overall judgment of each chapter or article by appropriate marks in the margins of the table of contents; for example, by checks: $\sqrt{}$, $\sqrt{-}$, or $\sqrt{+}$. Writing symbols in the table of contents can be helpful to you immediately and at many points in your professional future, up to the day when you decide to give away some of the books and journals you have accumulated through the years. All you will need to do is look for a $\sqrt{+}$ on the cover or the table of contents to decide whether you should keep the material.

d) In the margins of the table of contents, next to the titles of the portions you have read, write the page numbers and parts of pages you found especially valuable.

e) Photocopy pages that you must keep readily accessible. Also photocopy the title page, copyright notice, and table of contents, or note complete bibliographical information directly on the first or last page of each copy; you will need this information later if you want to cite the material or write for permission to use it. (See the appendix of this book for information about copyright laws, pages 129–133.) Determine the key word or subject under which you should file the pages and file them either temporarily in an alphabetized accordian file or permanently in indexed file folders or the like.

4. If you have accumulated quantities of books and journals but given them little more than a glance, bring yourself to read them by previewing, chunking, and selecting.

a) Preview and chunk: Look over all the books, group them by the subjects of concern to you, and subgroup them alphabetically by author.

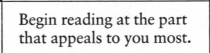

Begin reading at the part that appeals to you most.

b) Preview and select: Preview a few books that particularly appeal to you and select one of these to start reading as thoroughly as necessary. Begin reading at the part that appeals to you most, thus lessening any tendency you may have to procrastinate. Having started so well, you might feel inspired to move on to the next most appealing part, or to go back and read from the beginning, or to move on to a different book.

c) When you encounter a part that you especially want to remember, tell yourself or a companion about it from memory.

d) Keep a loose-leaf memo book in your pocket or pocketbook, one with pages the same size as the index cards you use regularly, so that you can note new ideas, information, or references immediately and can file the notes easily.

5. File your notes and photocopies systematically, for ready retrieval. Browse in a well-stocked stationery or office-supply store and buy various kinds of aids to filing, like these:

a) for short-term storage, when you are in a hurry, large accordion notebooks or envelopes, with alphabetic tabs, and file boxes with index cards and dividers;

b) for long-term storage, when you have time to file more carefully, containers of various types and sizes with self-stick labels—shelves, file drawers and cabinets, three-ring notebooks with dividers that have pockets;

c) for longest-term storage, when you want the materials to remain in good condition for as long as possible, acid-free containers, which are available through companies that sell archival material (museum or library personnel can refer you to these companies).

6. Exchange information and ideas with colleagues.

a) Participate in continuing education that may be provided in your workplace.

b) Initiate continuing education. For example, organize a discussion group for interested members of your profession and related fields.

c) Meet colleagues for lunch and informal exchange of information and ideas—including ideas about keeping up in your field or profession.

7. If and when you decide to change fields, cut back to part-time, or retire, enjoy additional fruits of lifelong learning.

a) Give away or sell books and journals that you no longer need and that others might find helpful.

1) If you haven't marked all over your books, they will be more readable by others, so that you can sell them or trade them, give them to friends, or contribute them (with an income tax deduction) to professional libraries. Some institutions have

sibling institutions, often ones in developing countries, for which gifts of books are welcome. An office of planned giving or international programs in the benefactor institution may take care of shipping the books.

2) If you decide to give away large numbers of books and journals, employ a librarian to list and assess them. Copies of such an assessment can give you an accurate record of your gift's value for income tax deductions; they can make your gift more useful to the institution to which you give them, and they can remind you of which books and journals you gave away, if you start looking for one in its former place in your library.

b) If you audit courses, join reading groups, or read extensively on your own, you may want to continue using methods that have helped you learn more in less time. Or you may simply want to enjoy reading without concern for how much you remember. More and more you may agree with Sir Francis Bacon in his essay "Of Studies": "Some books are to be tasted, others to be swallowed, and some few to be chewed and digested."

■ Keeping Better Informed Through Newspapers and Magazines

Keeping up with new information in your professional field, like keeping up with school assignments, is a major responsibility. You also have to keep well-informed for all the other roles you have, from family member to voter to volunteer. For all these responsibilities, there are many ways to learn more in less time.

Keeping yourself well-informed can seem like a never-ending chore or a pleasurable challenge, depending upon your attitude and the way you go about it. Educating yourself for the many purposes in your life usually requires more than reading headlines, skimming a few articles, listening to National Public Radio or other news-centered radio stations, and watching televised information programs. It requires continual and selective reading, discussing, storing, and reviewing.

Here are some ways to keep better informed and to feel less overwhelmed by all the new information that seems important to know and remember:

■ Read newspapers and magazines selectively

1. Evaluate the periodicals that you have been reading regularly. In addition to a local newspaper, do these periodicals include at least one other major newspaper and several different types of periodicals? Browse through a well-stocked periodical collection of a li-

brary or bookstore to find additional periodicals you might want to explore.

2. To develop and satisfy new interests, keep adding to and deleting from the periodicals that you read regularly. For example, if you become more concerned about maintaining your health, add a health newsletter, like the *University of California Berkeley Wellness Letter*, or the *Health Letter*, published by the Center for Science in the Public Interest.

3. Make some effort to impress upon your memory what you have read. The process can be like ways you remember pleasant events or vacations. On vacations you may take photographs, write postcards or letters, keep a journal, and bring home souvenirs. Later, you review your mementos and so refresh your memory and deepen your insights about your experiences. Similarly, to keep better informed about subjects of interest to you, save articles or whole issues of magazines and review them later.

4. To remember more of the information you have read, follow appropriate steps for previewing, selecting, chunking, and processing, which are described most fully in "Using Four Methods for Effective Study and Analogous Activities" (pages 75–76) and follow the appropriate steps described in "Reading rapidly for key ideas only" (pages 20–22).

5. As you engage in your work or other activities, consciously try to apply what you have learned from any material that you have read to keep informed. This will help you integrate the information more fully into your knowledge system and help you retrieve it more quickly when you need it.

■ Preview and select

1. When you start reading a newspaper, look at the first page to get an idea of the main news and features. If you do not have time to read all the sections immediately, look over the pages quickly, check the articles you want to read, and mark on the top of the first page

of each section the pages where the articles you've checked appear.

2. When you pick up a magazine, browse through the pages and mark in the margin of the table of contents the articles that you want to read.

3. Preview any article of interest to you, then read the article selectively if you decide you want to know more than you gained from the preview alone.

■ Select and chunk

When you are reading an article, bracket in the margin any lines or paragraphs of particular interest to you. If the article seems to you worth saving, note the number of the article's first page (like this, "p. 9 + ") on the front page of the newspaper, or on the cover or table of contents of the magazine. If you took this step when you first browsed through the newspaper or magazine, circle the page number after you have read the article and have decided to save it.

1. When you have finished reading a whole magazine or a whole section of a newspaper, mark a check (√) on the front of those you want to keep, and mark an X on any that you do not want to keep. Then, when trash or recycle day comes, you will not have to spend time deciding which magazines and newspapers to discard or save.

2. Tear out pages that include articles you want to read when you have more time, perhaps on train or plane rides or while waiting for someone. Collect them in a well-marked and sturdy folder that is easy to carry.

■ Process deeply

1. After you have read and marked an article, review immediately, from memory, whatever information you want to be sure to remember beyond tomorrow. To remember the information still better and longer, tell someone else about what you have read and discuss issues or questions raised in the material.

2. Develop a simple method for storing articles or magazines for a period of months. After many months, choose from your collection any materials that you think are worth keeping on file for years. This process can help you remember what you learned from all the articles, as well as help you make special articles accessible for future use.

■ Store selected articles, short-term or long-term

1. Before discarding a newspaper or magazine, look at the page numbers you have noted on the front page, cover, or table of contents. Tear out any pages you have noted that still seem worth keeping and store them in a box or drawer. At this point, do not spend time clipping out the articles from the pages. If there are any magazines that you want to save whole, put them aside on a special shelf.

2. At the top of your pile of newspaper and magazine pages or in a file drawer, keep folders for collecting articles on a few subjects of greatest interest to you, such as health, travel, or new books. This rough categorizing can save you time in several ways: It will make it easier to find an article about your main interests, and it will prevent you from accumulating too large a pile of unsorted articles.

3. Wait a year or so to clip out some of the articles. By then, you can decide quickly which articles you still want, and probably more than half of them will not seem worth saving any longer.

4. Your attitude about this whole process can affect how easy or difficult it seems. If you think of it as a way to refresh your memory, it will seem pleasant rather than tedious. If you think of it as part of an overall effort to keep better informed, you will not be so inclined to procrastinate. Starting with the following steps will help, too:

   a) Gather the supplies you will need: file folders and an accordion file, a trash basket, labels, scissors, a stapler, transparent tape for any torn pages, a colored pen, and your memorandum book or calendar.

b) Start clipping and filing from the group or pile of articles that has the most immediate priority or value for you. For example, you might want to retrieve articles on an aspect of health that is of particular importance to you.

c) Review the marked parts of each article, reconsidering their possible value for you or others. For all articles that you decide to save, write the name and date of the periodical on the first page, if this information is not printed there.

d) File these articles in an accordion file folder. Develop a table of contents for the folder and store it inside. Set aside any articles that you want to photocopy and/or share with others.

e) In the year or so after a clipping-and-filing session, whenever you need specific material that you placed temporarily in the accordion folder, transfer to a file folder the whole group of articles on that subject, for long-term storage in your home or office. In other words, transfer the articles from quick and temporary storage to long-term storage, one subject at a time, rather than attempting to file permanently all the materials about all the subjects at once.

f) For articles in whole magazines that you save, mark on the table of contents the page numbers and parts of pages ("87 B," "90 E") that you think are especially valuable (See "Saving Time in Taking Notes from Reading," pages 18–19). If the periodical provides an annual index of articles, mark in the index the articles you found most valuable.

> The whole process
> may become a
> kind of hobby
> for you.

■ Adapt your methods to your evolving interests and needs

As your interests and needs change, revise and reorganize your collection of articles:

1. Subcategorize your files and revise your tables of contents accordingly. If you realize that your main interests are health and travel, subcategorize these topics: divide "health" into subcategories like "nutrition" and "safety," and divide "travel" into subcategories like the different places you want to go.

   a) For "travel," for example, keep folders handy for filing material about the trips you are planning currently. Keep other travel material with files that you use less frequently.

   b) Use a notebook with dividers that have pockets, instead of file folders, to store brochures and other material about some subjects, such as "nearby places of interest, restaurants, and inns."

2. Compile a table of contents for all your files and note where you have stored them.

3. If you decide to do extensive research to keep yourself better informed about a subject, you can use the same methods that you have developed for your professional needs. For example, borrow or buy books on the subject, and arrange for a computer search for more articles.

■ Why bother with a system to keep yourself informed?

1. Your personal collection of articles, with your brackets and written comments, is a record of your particular interests, concerns, and tastes. It is not impersonal, like a printout of abstracts from a computer search of articles. (However, a printout of abstracts can be a useful addition to your collection, if you mark it up for your purposes.)

2. Reviewing your articles, when you weed out and store them, is a valuable way to remember them longer, be-

cause the process involves both ego and pleasure. It is like taking photographs when you are on vacation, then later sorting and mounting them. In fact, the whole process may become a kind of hobby for you.

3. Saving selected articles gives you a ready resource to tap for your many roles or purposes.

4. As you mark and save articles, you may realize that you are developing new interests and values, which can lead you to affiliate with new groups, enjoy new hobbies, or even explore new careers.

■ Bibliography

The following books are recommended as additional sources of ideas or encouragement for improving reading, writing, and study. See also the bibliographies in the sections "Reading fiction or poetry for full effect and meaning" (page 34) and "Improving Writing" (page 89).

These books are likely to be available in libraries, university bookstores, and some general bookstores. If not, bookstores may order them for you, or you may order them directly by calling the publisher's 800 number (obtainable by dialing information, 800-555-1212).

Barnet, Sylvan. *A Short Guide to Writing about Art.* 3rd ed. Glenview, IL: Scott Foresman, 1988.

Burns, David D. *Feeling Good: The New Mood Therapy.* New York: New American Library, 1981.

Gibaldi, Joseph, and Walter S. Achtert, eds. *MLA Handbook for Writers of Research Papers, Theses and Dissertations.* 3rd ed. New York: Modern Language Association, 1988.

Lakein, Alan. *How to Get Control of Your Time and Your Life.* New York: New American Library, 1974, reprinted 1989.

Mann, Thomas. *A Guide to Library Research Methods.* New York: Oxford University Press, 1990.

Millman, Jason, and Walter Pauk. *How to Take Tests.* New York: McGraw-Hill, 1969.

Pauk, Walter. *How to Study in College.* 4th ed. Boston: Houghton Mifflin, 1989.

Publication Manual of the American Psychological Association. 3rd ed. Washington, DC: American Psychological Association, 1983.

Ronstadt, Ronald. *The Art of Case Analysis: A Guide to the Diagnosis of Business Situations.* 2nd ed. Dover, MA: Lord, 1980.

■ Appendix

■ Copyright Law: An Increasing Concern of Students and Professionals

The main purpose of copyright laws has been to protect the rights of authors and artists and their publishers, for the ultimate benefit of the public. In the United States, the first federal copyright law, which was enacted by Congress in 1790, emphasized "authors." It protected books, maps, and charts against printing, reprinting, publishing, and vending by unauthorized persons. Over the years, additional classes of works have been added and exclusive rights have been expanded.

The doctrine of Fair Use, which originated in the 1840s, limits the rights of authors, artists, and publishers, by allowing certain kinds of copying that are not considered infringements of the law. The current interpretation of Fair Use and a few other provisions of recent copyright laws are explained briefly in the excerpts below, from Harry G. Henn's *Henn on Copyright Law: A Practitioner's Guide*, 3rd ed. (New York: Practising Law Institute, 1991).

Caution regarding unauthorized copying or copyright infringement will become increasingly important, because in March 1989 the United States joined, at last, the Bern Union—Union Internationale pour la Protection des Œuvres Littéraires et Artistiques. This is a hundred-year-old international union of more than sixty countries, with headquarters in Bern, Switzerland. Each country belonging to the union grants citizens of other member countries the same copyright privileges as its own citizens. Although the United States has not acceded to all the provisions of the Bern convention, copyright law will be increasingly significant, in view of the added protection afforded to authors and publishers when a country becomes a signatory to the Bern convention.

It should not be overlooked that copyright law protects only original expression, not facts, regardless of how much effort was made to locate the facts. The Supreme Court of the United States, in an important decision in March 1991, held:

> Facts, whether alone or as part of a compilation, are not original and therefore may not be copyrighted. A factual compilation is eligible for copyright if it features an original selection or arrangement of facts, but the copyright is limited to the particular selection or arrangement. In no event may copyright extend to the facts themselves.

For more information about current copyright law in the United States, write or call the Copyright Office in the Library of Congress, to request its free packet of informational materials (which, like all U.S. Government materials, are not copyrighted). The address of the Copyright Office is 101 Independence Avenue SE, Washington, DC 20540; the telephone number is 202-479-0700. If you need specific legal advice, especially about copying material created by citizens of countries other than your own, consult an attorney.

When in doubt about using any copyrighted material, always write to the publisher, at least three months in advance of when you need to use the material, for permission to copy it. Be sure to describe or list the pages you want to copy, your intended audience, and your purposes. The permissions editor will tell you whether or not you can have permission to copy the material and the conditions involved, in particular the form of the acknowledgment that will be necessary and the fee, if any.

Excerpts from *Henn on Copyright Law: A Practitioner's Guide*, 3rd ed. by Harry G. Henn (New York: Practising Law Institute, 1991):

FAIR USE

In General

The 1976 Act provided no definitions of fair use [one of the exceptions to the copyright law], but suggests criteria. Whether a use is fair depends upon:

1. The "purpose" of the use; and
2. At least four "factors."

Purposes

Use can be "fair" for "purposes" "such as" criticism, comment, news reporting, teaching (including multiple copies for classroom use), scholarship, or research. [pp. 227–229]

Factors

In determining whether the use "in any particular case" is a fair use, the "factors" to be considered shall "include":

1. The "purpose" and "character" of the use, including whether such use is of a "commercial nature" or is "for nonprofit educational purposes";
2. The "nature" of the copyrighted work;
3. The "amount and substantiality of the portion used" in relation to the copyrighted work as a whole; and
4. The effect of the use upon the "potential market for or value of" the copyrighted work. . . . [pp. 230–231]

This fourth factor, "the effect of the use upon the potential market for or value of the copyrighted work," "is undoubtedly the single most important element of fair use."[p. 234]

• • •

Classroom Copying of Books and Periodicals

The guidelines for classroom copying in not-for-profit educational institutions with respect to books and periodicals were prepared by representatives of the Ad Hoc Committee of Educational Institutions and Organizations on Copyright Law Revision, the Authors League of America, Inc., and the Association of American Publishers, Inc. Although not binding, the guidelines significantly influence courts, and have the practical impact of statutory provisions.

Single Copies

A teacher may reproduce a *single* copy, subject to "prohibitions," for research or teaching purposes, of:

1. A chapter from a book;
2. An article from a periodical or newspaper;
3. A short story, short essay, or short poem, whether or not from a collective work;
4. A chart, graph, diagram, drawing, cartoon, or picture from a book, periodical, or newspaper. [p. 237]

Multiple Copies

A teacher may make *multiple* copies for classroom use if the copying meets certain tests for brevity, spontaneity, and cumulative effect. Each copy must also include a notice of copyright. [pp. 237–238]

Prohibitions

Prohibitions applicable to both single and multiple copying are:

1. The copies may not be used for anthologies, compilations, or collective works;
2. "Consumable" materials, such as workbooks, tests, and answer sheets, may not be copied;
3. Copying may not be used to substitute for purchasing, be "directed by higher authority," or be repeated "with respect to the same item by the same teacher from term to term";
4. The student may not be charged more than the actual costs of the photocopying. [pp. 238–239]

• • •

REPRODUCTION AND DISTRIBUTION BY LIBRARIES AND ARCHIVES

Conditions

The rights of reproduction and distribution of a library or archives, or any of its employees acting within the scope of their employment, are limited to "no more than one copy or phonorecord of a work" and are subject to three specified overall conditions: [p. 250]

1. The making must be "without any purpose of direct or indirect commercial advantage";
2. The collections of the library or archives must be open to the public or available not only to affiliated researchers but also to other persons "doing research in a specialized field"; and
3. The reproduction or distribution must include a "notice of copyright." [p. 251]

Liability of User of Reproducing Equipment or Requester of Copies or Phonorecords

Liability for copyright infringement of a person who uses the reproducing equipment in a library or archive or who requests copies or phonorecords of articles or other contributions to a copyrighted collection or periodical issue or of a small part of any other copyrighted work for any such act, or for any later use of such copy or phonorecord, if it exceeds fair use, is not excused by the libraries-and-archives provisions. [pp. 260–261]

• • •

Future Prospects

There are growing disputes between publishers and authors, on the one hand, and librarians and educators, on the other.

A private Copyright Clearance Center (CCC) was established in 1978 to collect fees from photocopiers and to divide the proceeds among copyright owners. In 1984, the Center began to issue blanket licenses under a contract fee based on statistical samples for periodicals and journals ("Annual Authorization Service"). As a result, increased numbers of corporations have subscribed. The Center has been denied tax-exempt status. [p. 263]

More Books for Writers, Students, and Businesspeople

THINKERTOYS
A Handbook of Business Creativity for the 90s
by Michael Michalko
This book shows how anyone can become more creative and provides dozens of proven techniques for generating innovative ideas for new businesses, products, sales techniques, markets, and so on.
$16.95 paper, 360 pages

GRADUATE ADMISSIONS ESSAYS
What Works, What Doesn't, and Why
by Donald Asher
The author of *Overnight Resume* checks in with effective writing techniques that will allow anyone to craft an impressive essay—overnight. Based on interviews with admissions officers at top schools, it includes samples of their favorite essays.
$9.95 paper, 128 pages

FROM COLLEGE TO CAREER
Entry-Level Resumes for Any Major
by Donald Asher
Real-world examples illustrate techniques for showing all academic and job experience (or lack thereof) in the best light.
$7.95 paper, 128 pages

COLLEGE DEGREES BY MAIL
by John Bear
It is possible to earn good, legitimate, useable bachelor's, master's, doctorate, and law degrees entirely through home study—in as short as three months and for as little as $500. Bear describes 100 of the best schools and gives valuable information on exams, honorary degrees, and credit for life experience.
$12.95 paper, 160 pages

FINDING MONEY FOR COLLEGE
by John Bear
More than $6.5 billion in student loans goes unclaimed
each year. This book shows how to find out about and use
those loans. Also covers private foundations, grants, and
creative, nontraditional ways to fund an education.
$7.95 paper, 168 pages

Available from your local bookstore, or order direct from
the publisher. Please include $2 shipping and handling for
the first book, plus 50 cents for each additional book. California residents should include local sales tax. Write for our
free complete catalog of more than 400 books, posters, and
tapes.

Ten Speed Press
Box 7123
Berkeley, CA 94707

For Mastercard and VISA orders, call (510) 845-8414